GUNSMOKE

Also by Joseph G. Rosa

They Called Him Wild Bill: The Life and Adventures of James Butler Hickok
Alias Jack McCall
The Gunfighter: Man or Myth?
The Pleasure of Guns (*with Robin May*)

Also by Robin May

The American West (*with G. A. Embleton*)
Wolfe's Army (*with G. A. Embleton*)
The British Army in the American Revolution 1775-1783 (*with G. A. Embleton*)
The Wild West

GUNSMOKE

A STUDY OF VIOLENCE IN THE WILD WEST

JOSEPH G. ROSA
and ROBIN MAY

NEW ENGLISH LIBRARY
TIMES MIRROR

For Nyle H. Miller, Joseph W. Snell and Tim Bannon, Kansans all

First published in Great Britain by New English Library, Barnard's Inn, Holborn, London EC1N 2JR in 1977

Designed by Oliver Hickey

Printed in Great Britain by
Thomson Litho Ltd, East Kilbride, Scotland.

Bound by Hunter & Foulis, Edinburgh.

4500 32752

CONTENTS

ACKNOWLEDGEMENTS

The authors would like to thank the following for permission to reproduce the photographs which appear in this book. Figures in bold type refer to the colour section. Arizona Historical Society Library: 44; Amon Carter Museum of Western Art: **3, 8**; Collection in the Museum of New Mexico: 15-17, 35; Columbia Pictures Corporation Ltd: 108; Denver Public Library, Western History Department: 11, 36, 39, 65, 89, 102; Pat Hall: 21; the Harmson Collection of Western Art: **2**; Ethel Hickok: 88; the Kansas State Historical Society, Topeka: 1, 14, 34, 56-7, 66-74, 77, 87, 90-4, 96, 103, Appendix 2, 1-13; Robin May Collection: 2, 7, 9, 12, 44, 47-50, 59, 76, 98, 104; Minnesota Historical Society: 28-30; Montana Historical Society, Helena: 10, 40-1; Oklahoma Historical Society: 86; Pinkerton's National Detective Agency Inc: 51; Private Collection: **4, 5, 6, 7, 9, 10, 11**; Joseph G. Rosa Western Americana Collection: 18-20, 31, 38, 46, 58, 61-4, 75, 78-85, 95, 97, 99-101, 105-7, 109-12, Appendix 1, 1-8, **1**; St Joseph Museum, St Joseph, Missouri: 25-6; Secretary of the Interior, the National Archives: 13; State Historical Society of Missouri: 27; US Signal Corps, the National Archives: 8, 31, 43, 52, 55; Wells Fargo Bank History Room, San Francisco: 54; Western History Collections, University of Oklahoma Library: 33, 37, 42, 47, 53; Western University Research Center, University of Wyoming: 22-4, 45; Wyoming State Archives and Historical Dept: 3, 60.

INTRODUCTION

Whenever you get into a row be sure and not shoot too quick. I've known many a feller slip up for shootin' in a hurry.
Wild Bill Hickok, 1865

It was an epic era of blood, guts and glory that bred rugged men and inspired legends; a moment in history that magnified the deeds of characters as diverse as cowboys, Indians, soldiers, pioneers and trappers. But dominating this colourful and – at a distance – romantic crew was that half man, half mythical embodiment of the good, the bad and the ungodly that today we call the gunfighter.

In legend he resembles the cowboy that he rarely was – a buckskin-clad Sir Galahad of the plains, whose weapon, a .45 calibre Colt revolver, was always cocked and ready to defend the weak and helpless against all evil.

In battle he is an eye-catching figure in the noonday sun awaiting the moment when his enemy will make the fatal move to draw his pistol. The silence is shattered by an ear-splitting roar, and when the gunsmoke clears, he stands alone, as the eager undertakers move in to remove yet another dead villain.

That is how Hollywood for over seventy years, and novels for even longer, have depicted the gunfighter. Is the picture fictional? A figment of a writer's imagination? Partly, perhaps. Yet the truth is that the Old West was wild, and men did shoot it out on the streets, in saloons, and all over the vast area beyond the Mississippi and the wide Missouri. Lawmen and outlaws frequently resorted to gunfights, and statistics suggest that between 1866 and 1900 some 20,000 men died of lead poisoning. Many were killed in Texas and other turbulent Southern states in the post Civil War era, when the hated Reconstruction policy and family feuds accounted for innumerable deaths.

1
Dressed in a buckskin suit trimmed with fur, James Butler 'Wild Bill' Hickok poses impressively, armed with a pair of Colt's 1851 Model 'Navy' revolvers and what appears to be a plains butcher's knife of the Bowie type. The pistols are carried in conventional plains-style, with butts forward for a reverse, or twist, draw. The knife is thought to be a prop. The portrait probably dates from 1865.

The men we now call gunfighters came from every walk of life, and their approach to their lethal trade differed from individual to individual. But this deadly brotherhood of the gun shared one common characteristic that set them apart from other Westerners; they were killers. Their environment helped make them and their actions were dictated by circumstances.

It is impossible to guess now if these men regarded themselves in the same light as we do today. Certainly, they were well aware of their effect on frontier society. In their own time they were usually described as 'shootists' (which also meant marksmen) or 'man-killers'. The generic word 'gunfighter' is more modern, but it can be traced back at least to 1874 when an obnoxious self-named individual called Cemetery Sam informed the inhabitants of a saloon in Eureka, California, that he was a gunfighter. No one took him seriously, in fact someone promptly knocked him down. Not until our own century was the word 'gunfighter' used to describe the lawman, or 'good man', while the more sinister term 'gunman' came to epitomise the 'bad man'.

To distinguish further between the two, Edgar Beecher Bronson in his *The Red-blooded Heroes of the Frontier*, published in 1910, remarked that there were two types of man-killers and these were sub-divided into classes:

> The first types numbered all who took life in contravention of the law. This type was divided into three classes: A. Outlaws to whom blood-letting had become a mania: B. Outlaws who killed in defense of their spoils or their liberty: C. Otherwise good men who had slain in the heat of private quarrel, and either 'gone on the scout' or 'jumped the country' rather than submit to arrest.

The second type included all those who slew in support of law and order. The editor of the Kansas City *Journal*, 15 November 1881, in describing the gentleman who had 'killed his man', noted that he looked very ordinary:

> He may be found behind the bar in a Main Street saloon; he may be seen by an admiring audience doing the pedestal clog at a variety theater; his special forte may be driving a cab, or he may be behind the rosewood counters of a bank. If he has been here any great number of years, his 'man' was probably a Pioneer, and died in the interest of 'law and order' – at least so the legend runs. And no one dares dispute the verity of the legend, for behold the man who executed a violator of the law without waiting for the silly formalities of a judge and jury, mayhap now sits in a cushioned pew at an aristocratic church, and prays with a regularity, grace and precision only equalled by his unerring aim with a revolver, the great Western civilizer.

2
Frederick Remington's 'A Fight in the Street'.

Most of the men who achieved some sort of notoriety in the West came from comparatively 'civilised' areas. Wild Bill Hickok, 'Rowdy Joe' Lowe, Wyatt Earp and Bat Masterson (who was born in Canada) all moved to Kansas from Illinois; Sam Bass was from Indiana, and Billy the Kid was probably from New York State.

It has been claimed that the gunfighter was 'born' in Kansas and grew up among the early Kansas-Missouri Border wars which

3
The date is 1872, the place Sawtell's Ranch. The impressive wall decorations need no comment.

preceded the Civil War, and that he matured during the great cattle drives northwards out of Texas in the 1860s and 1870s. This is only partly true, for the man with the gun was equally as industrious in Missouri, in Arizona, Montana and most of California. The gold rushes of the Far West knew him, and so did mining and logging camps, and everywhere he went he made his mark.

The gunfighter's skill with a pistol is legendary, and for some it was indeed a profession. But it was also a state of mind. Skill in the handling and use of weapons, and the ability to shoot fast and accurately at a moving target counted for a lot, but without co-ordination of mind and muscle, the nerve and the instinct to kill or be killed at all times, the fastest man on the draw would have been useless in a gunfight.

It was these factors that placed the gunfighter far and away above his gun-toting companions on the trail or in a frontier town. A good gunfighter knew his limitations and never tried to overstep them. Speed counted little in a gunfight. It was the man that took his time, placed his shot and made sure of his target who won, not the flashy trick shooters who relied on speed.

The choice of weapons varied. In the early days, percussion revolvers, which had to be loaded with powder and ball and percussion cap, one chamber at a time, were the favourite weapons; but later, with the introduction of metallic ammunition, the Colt Single Action (which meant that it had to be thumb-cocked for each shot) .45 calibre model of 1873 was the most popular pistol. By the late 1870s, the same weapon was available in

4
Wild Bill Hickok and Dave Tutt fall out, as seen by Harper's New Monthly Magazine.

.44-40 calibre as well, the same calibre that was used in the famous Winchester rifle, model of 1873. Barrel lengths also varied, but the preferred lengths were the standard $7\frac{1}{2}$in or $5\frac{1}{2}$in.

Some men worked on the actions of their pistols so that when they were cocked the lightest pull on the trigger tripped the hammer, while others removed the trigger altogether and relied upon the thumb to cock and fire the pistol in one movement. But whatever the gunfighter's preference for pistols might be, he was primed for action.

Curiously, few Western gunfights took place between individuals who were equally matched. The top-liners rarely had to prove themselves to each other. For the most part, problems were caused by those eager to prove that they were their equals, and the easiest way to provoke such a fight was over wine, women and cards. This meant that a man with a reputation was constantly forced to defend it to stay alive.

The actual gunfight, the climax of most books and films, is usually depicted as a face-to-face duel in the sun. Avid Western fans regard the gunfight at the OK Corral as the classic encounter, which took place in Tombstone, Arizona, on 26 October 1881, when the Earp gang fought it out with the Clantons and McLaurys. The fans may well be forgiven for assuming that this notorious, still controversial, fight inspired the immortal Western 'walk and draw' gunfight, but it did not.

The gunfight that set the pattern for the legendary version took place fourteen years before on 21 July 1865, at Springfield, Missouri, between David Tutt, an ex-Confederate soldier, and the man who today is regarded as the epitome of the Western gunfighter, James Butler 'Wild Bill' Hickok. On that day both men made history, for their brief encounter was a classic. Both were

5
Wild Bill challenges friends of the deceased.

skilled pistol shots, and courageous enough to shoot while being shot at. They had quarrelled over cards, and probably a woman, and Tutt had taken Hickok's watch and threatened to wear it on the square. Hickok advised him against it, adding that he could wear the watch if 'dead men can walk', but Tutt ignored him.

Shortly after 6pm, Tutt appeared on Market Square and Hickok started walking towards him. Both men were equally matched, primed and ready for action. When they were about fifty yards apart, Tutt drew his pistol and fired. He missed. Before he could recock it, Hickok had drawn his and fired – once. Tutt fell with a bullet through the heart.

Immediately Wild Bill spun on his heel and pointed his pistol at a group of Tutt's friends who stood behind him.

'Aren't you satisfied, gentlemen?' he asked. 'Put up your shootin'-irons, or there'll be more dead men here.' Muttering among themselves they obeyed and slowly dispersed, leaving him alone on the square.

Hickok was promptly arrested but was allowed bail. Soon afterwards he went on trial, but was acquitted on his plea of self-defence.

For every gunfighter who took his time and placed his shots, there were others who neglected the basic rules and died because of it. Charlie Harrison was a gambler from St Louis who had a reputation as a good man in a fight, but when he shot it out with gambler Jim Levy one night in Cheyenne, Wyoming, in March 1877, he fired in a hurry and missed. Levy did not. But Jim then proceeded to mar his reputation by deliberately shooting his opponent as he lay on the ground before turning and walking away. Harrison died two weeks later and the local press condemned Levy's plea of self-defence and suggested that the 'pistoliferous gambler' should suffer the severest penalty of the law; but his friends secured his release on bail and he disappeared.

All over the West men fought and died, sometimes for trivial reasons, and those with reputations were always prime targets. Bob Ford, 'the dirty little coward', as a contemporary song dubbed him, shot his cousin Jesse James both for the reward money and because he yearned for the reputation of being the man who had killed him. But ten years later he, too, was the victim, killed by a man who wanted to be known as 'the man who killed the man who killed Jesse James'! And so it went on. There was always someone anxious to don the dangerous mantle of reputation no matter what the cost.

The 'good bad man' that inspired the gunfighter was always a controversial figure. One day he might be regarded as law-abiding and respected by his fellow citizens, and perhaps employed as a peace officer, the next he was liable to be a social outcast, a vagrant, a pariah shunned by those same citizens.

In the chapters that follow, great reliance has been placed on contemporary material such as old newspapers, court records and official documents as well as the comparatively few trustworthy printed sources. These, together with a large number of contemporary photographs will, we hope, depict the old-time gunfighter as he really was, set against the backdrop of the vast, epic panorama that was the Old West.

Joseph G. Rosa
Robin May
London, 1977

6
This impressive gentleman is 'Wild Ben' Raymond, an early-day character of Leadville, Dakota Territory, photographed about 1879. He carried two .44 Merwin and Hulbert pistols 'cross draw' fashion, one of which is in an open-topped holster and the other in a conventional flap holster of the type mostly used by the US Army.

1 THE VIOLENT WEST

The first twenty-six graves in the Virginia [City] cemetery were occupied by murdered men. So everybody said, so everybody believed, and so they will always say and believe.
Mark Twain *Roughing It*

A wildly improbable tale has it that one Saint Brendan was the first white man to reach America some time in the sixth century. Presumably, the sailor-saint was non-violent, unlike the Norsemen who followed him around 1000 AD, landing in Newfoundland, possibly on the eastern seaboard of what is now the United States, and calling their discovery Vinland. If their Icelandic sagas are to be believed, and few now doubt their essential truth, the tradition of white violence in America was begun by Thorvald, brother of the first man to reach Vinland, Leif Ericson. Seeing three humps in the sand, which turned out to be canoes, each with three Skraelings (Indians) under them, he and his men promptly killed all except one of them, and Thorvald was repaid by a mortal wound from an arrow.

So in their very first encounter blood had been shed between red man and white. The Indians had arrived on foot from Asia by way of the Bering Strait from around 30,000 BC onwards and fought innumerable and unrecorded inter-tribal battles.

Gunsmoke reached America with the Spaniards, who also brought genocide on a scale never matched by anyone, for soon after Columbus's landfall in 1492 in the West Indies, they killed almost the entire Carib people by savage overwork or worse, leaving nothing to recall them but an evocative word, Caribbean. Next the Spaniards, in small, daring bands, conquered Mexico and Peru, then, in 1540, headed north out of Mexico under Coronado into the trans-Mississippi West, the 'real' West. Coronado and his iron-hard men headed northwards lusting after gold, and they reached what is now Kansas before returning, leaving a bloody trail behind them.

It is hardly surprising, therefore, that the American nation, which was itself to be born in violence, grew to maturity on it, and is today steeped in its traditions, and gun conscious to a remarkable degree.

In the wake of the Spaniards came the French, Dutch and English, and, despite the building of settlements and the introduction of laws from the mother countries, violence between white and white, and white and red was inevitable. And many of those who had fled from the persecutions, restrictions and deprivations of the Old World, still felt restless enough to edge into the only general direction left them – westwards.

By the nineteenth century the Frontier West – that vast region extending from the Appalachian Mountains out across the Great Plains, and over the Rocky Mountains and Sierras to the Pacific – was still only sparsely populated by mainly nomadic and semi-nomadic tribes. Their way of life had now been transformed by the coming of the horse from the east and, especially, from the south west, where Spain had a thin string of outposts which stretched as far as California. There may have been a million Indians; there were certainly millions of buffalo.

Those who ventured across the Appalachians from the 1770s were used enough to the terrors of forest warfare. This, and not the 1860s, was the time when white men first said: 'The only good Indian is a dead one' and – to justify baby-killing – 'Nits make lice'. Racial tension flared mainly because of white land hunger followed by Indian revenge. Atrocity bred atrocity, and, though the eastern seaboard, relieved of fear from the French and, finally, of British rule, settled down, the Frontier, moving slowly westwards, remained a land fraught with danger and sudden death. There were outlaws in the wild Ohio country and the woods of Tennessee in the 1790s and early 1800s who make their counterparts of the 1860s to the 1890s, even dedicated killers like John Wesley Hardin, seem like sober citizens.

The Louisiana Purchase of 1803 from France, which doubled the size of the United States at a stroke of a pen, giving her the entire region from the Mississippi basin to the Rockies, triggered off ex-

7
Frederick Remington's 'The Trapper'. From around 1810 to the 1840s, when beaver fur went out of fashion, men like this – Mountain Men – roamed the West, blazing trails, living like Indians, fighting Indians, marrying them. They were the toughest Westerners of them all.

peditions to a region into which few whites – a handful of traders and trappers – had penetrated. The Government-sponsored Lewis and Clark expedition of 1804 to 1806 was the first to cross it to the Pacific and back, and others followed. From around 1810 to 1830 the fabulous Mountain Men blazed trails across the West as they searched for beaver, whose fur was high fashion in the East, and in Britain and Europe. These 'white Indians', who fought with, lived with and married Indians, lived and often died violently. Some of them, notably Jim Bridger, Kit Carson and Jedediah Smith, remain American legends.

But it was from the South that the cult of violence spread most widely to the West. In the southern states there was a tradition of duelling ranging from gentlemanly shoot-outs with pistols to savage knife fights and brawling in which gouging out the opponent's eyes was only one speciality.

Texas, into which Anglo-Americans began to migrate in the 1820s when it was still Mexican (Mexico having freed itself from Spain in 1821), broke away violently from its rulers under the leadership of Samuel Houston, an ex-Governor of Tennessee, who fought Indians, loved Indians, Indian girls and drink, and was one of the most remarkable men of his age. He was given time to save his adopted country by the defenders of the immortal Alamo, including Jim 'the Knife' Bowie and Davy 'the Hat' Crockett and others who died in truly glorious circumstances, as did many more of their valiant enemies, in 1836.

With Texas independent, by 1840 the newly formed Texas Rangers, armed with Samuel Colt's new five-shot revolvers, were disputing the boundaries of the state with the Comanches, the Lords of the South Plains. And meanwhile, an uneasy co-existence reigned between Mexico and Texas until 1846, when the United States went to war with the former. Texans were happily annexed to the Union, and California was also taken over, becoming part of the United States by treaty in 1848 after it had already been seized by force.

The discovery of gold in California just before the peace treaty was signed led to the greatest of all gold rushes; a population explosion – there were only 14,000 whites in California before the rush; and statehood in 1850, despite the fact that between Californians and the settlements along the Missouri were 2000 miles of wilderness, an area loosely and wrongly described as the Great American Desert. Reliable information on this region was so lacking that although thousands had gone west along the Oregon and California Trails prior to the American Civil War, even after it had ended in 1865, many thought that the 'desert' was arid and worthless, fit only for buffalo and for banished tribes from the East, who could share it with the roving Plains Indians.

California's contribution to the violent West was inevitable and notable. Once gold fever had gripped men, and women, from all over the world, people of every race and class invaded the region and racial tension built up rapidly. Native Californians, mostly of Mexican origin, were relegated to second-class citizens, along with other Latins, and Chinese emigrants were persecuted. As for California's mainly peaceable and backward Indians, they were almost exterminated.

After the first year, 1848, when conditions on the goldfields were almost idyllic in what was essentially a local rush, the rapid build-up of population as the Forty-Niners and their successors flocked to the goldfields, meant that the need to establish law and order became urgent. English law, which was the basis for the laws in most Eastern states, was difficult to apply to the Far West, where areas not even classed as territories, let alone states, found that they could expect little help from the Government in Washington. So those who cared were forced to make their own laws. It was then, in California and elsewhere, that vigilante law came into its own.

The actions of the vigilantes, frequently spur-of-the-moment reactions to crimes and criminals, were frowned on by more settled societies, but were usually a lesser evil than complete lawlessness. This was particularly evident on the frontier, where population swiftly outpaced organised government. In booming San Francisco, a village of only 800 people in 1847, in the Californian gold camps, in Idaho, Montana, Colorado, Nevada and the Dakotas, there was near anarchy to begin with, and a curious toleration of law-breaking, partly because everyone was busy with the main concern, trying to make money. But soon sterner measures were called for, and the 'rope justice' or 'hemp justice' of 'Judge Lynch and his midnight court' was swiftly called into action.

'Lynch's law' is claimed by some to have originated with one John Lynch, the founder of Lynchburg, Virginia; other accounts suggest that it was Major John Fitzstephen Lynch of Galway, Ireland, who ordered the execution of his own son; but according to some

8

John Heath, victim of an Arizona lynch mob at Tombstone in 1884, typifies the macabre use members of the 'Uplift Society' made of telegraph poles.

historians the term was originated in the 1780s by one Colonel Charles Lynch. He and his neighbours of Bedford County, Virginia, took it upon themselves to punish horse-thieves and others when the law failed to act. Each man had the chance to plead his case and if proved innocent was set free. If found guilty, however, he could expect a savage beating and banishment from the country. Soon other parts of Virginia adopted 'Lynch's law'; but only later did Lynch law acquire its more sinister association with sudden death.

The vigilantes wasted little time in explanation when they set out to track down murderers and horse-thieves, and some regarded their activities with considerable alarm. A report published in the London *Morning Chronicle* on 3 September 1851, noted that:

> If the state of society in California demands the existence of a 'Committee of Vigilance,' the action of that body should be in co-operation with the officers of justice. Acting in defiance of the law, it perpetrates abuses more dangerous than those which it seeks to remedy. The defenders of this association point to its rapid increase in numbers as an evidence of its popularity. No wonder that people aspire to enrol themselves on its lists. It is the supreme power in the State. Its control is unlimited. Life, liberty, property, and reputation are at its mercy. In the language of the local judiciary, it 'over-rides the law and sets the constitution at defiance.' Its organisation is extending itself by branches throughout the whole of California.

But not everyone thought that the vigilantes were a danger. In San Francisco and elsewhere they were reputable citizens, though in some places they wore masks and were little better than assassins. In many regions, reputable or not, they were the only law.

Law and order only took effect slowly in the West, and those hardy enough to survive the wilderness, the loneliness, the weather and the rigours of a semi-civilised existence were equally capable of taking care of

9

A few days before this warning was published, Frank, William and Simeon Reno, and Charlie Anderson, bank- and train-robbers, were brutally lynched in a 'night of blood' at New Albany Jail, Indiana.

HEADQUARTERS SOUTHERN INDIANA,

VIGILANCE COMMITTEE.

TO THE PEOPLE OF THE UNITED STATES!

"SALUS POPULI SUPREMA LEX."

WHEREAS, it became necessary for this organization to meet out summary punishment to the leaders of the thieves, robbers, murderers and desperadoes, who for many years defied law and order, and threatened the lives and property of honest citizens of this portion of Indiana, and as the late fearful tragedy at New Albany testifies that justice is slow, but sure, we promulgate this our pronunciamento, for the purpose of justifying to the world, and particularly to the people of the State of Indiana, any future action which we may take.

We deeply deplore the necessity which called our organization into existence; but the laws of our State are so defective that as they now stand on the Statute Books, they all favor criminals going unwhipt of justice; a retrospective view will show that in this respect we speak only the truth.

Having first lopped off the branches, and finally uprooted the tree of evil which was in our midst, in defiance of us and our laws, we beg to be allowed to rest here, and be not forced again to take the law into our own hands. We are very loth to shed blood again, and will not do so unless compelled in defence of our lives.

A WARNING.

We are well aware that at the present time, a combination of the few remaining thieves, their friends and sympathizers, has been formed against us, and have threatened all kinds of vengeance against persons whom they suppose to belong to this organization. They threaten assassination in every form, and that they will commit arson in such ways as will defy legal detection. The carrying out in whole, or in part, of each or any of these designs, is the only thing that will again cause us to rise in our own defence. The following named persons are solemnly warned, that their designs and opinions are known, and that they cannot, unknown to us, make a move toward retaliation.

Wilk Reno, Clinton Reno, Trick Reno, James Greer, Stephen Greer, Fee Johnson, Chris. Price, Harvey Needham, Meade Fislar, Mart Lowe, Roland Lee, William Sparks, Jesse Thompson, William Hare, William Biggers, James Fislar, Pollard Able.

If the above named individuals desire to remain in our midst, to pursue honest callings, and otherwise conduct themselves as law abiding citizens, we will protect them always.—If however, they commence their devilish designs against us, our property, or any good citizen of this district, we will rise but *once* more; do not trifle with us; for if you do, we will follow you to the bitter end; and give you a "short shrift and a hempen collar." As to this, our actions in the past, will be a guarantee for our conduct in the future.

We trust this will have a good effect. We repeat, we are very loth again to take life, and hope we shall never more be necessitated to take the law into our own hands.

By order of the Committee.

Dec. 21, 1868.

miscreants. And being the men they were, they injected a macabre humour into their attitude towards criminals whose lives were forfeit.

Old-timers wryly remarked that the favourite reading among vigilantes was the coroner's reports they inspired. Gleefully they recalled that many a guest of honour at a meeting of the 'Uplift Society' had been known to expire when the platform upon which he had been standing suddenly collapsed. In Western parlance a man was never 'hanged', he was 'hung' and a variety of cold-blooded but colourful expressions described the event: 'a suspended sentence' or 'a long stretch' to name but two; and for the religious-minded among them – 'jerked to Jesus'!

10
The Hangman's Tree at Helena, Montana, complete with occupants.

This strange mixture of comedy and the macabre came about mainly because of boredom, and published references, while amusing, do not disguise the root cause. In 1880, a gentleman calling himself 'Meredith, MD', arrived in Dodge City, Kansas, and announced that he was to give a lecture on certain 'private diseases', their prevention and cure. The meeting took place in the Lady Gay dance hall, and Bat Masterson, the erstwhile sheriff of Ford County, was asked to act as chairman. The proceedings came to an abrupt halt when someone in the audience started a fight. Masterson rushed forward to restore order, and drawing what was described by the local press as a 'Colt's improved, nickel plated, size 44 shooting instrument' formed himself into a 'hollow square in front of the horrified Doctor, determined to defend or die!' The lights went out, shots were fired, and when order was finally restored, Bat looked anxiously for his charge. He found him crouching under the speaker's stand, unharmed but scared out of his wits, with a bullet hole through the crown of his hat.

Like promoters of cock-fights, men deliberately put one man against another in the hope that they would see some action. Cowboys were known to relieve the boredom of the trail drive by slipping a rattlesnake into the bedding of some unsuspecting unfortunate, sometimes with tragic results. In 1896, it was reported by the Oberlin, Kansas *Herald* that

THE HARPES

In the 1780s, with the young United States finally free of the Mother Country, outlawry was already rife. It had flourished on the fringe of the war zones throughout the Revolution, and now a plague of armed bands took to highway robbery, horse-thieving and murder. Leading lights among the outlaw fraternity were the horrifying Harpes; Micajah, known as 'Big', and his brother Wiley, or Little Harpe. They came from North Carolina and, like others of Highland descent, had sided, as much as they sided with anyone, with the Crown against the Rebels in the war.

At first their post-war exploits were confined to robbery, interspersed with farming, but they soon found horse-stealing to be far more profitable. Then they switched to the more dangerous but much more lucrative profession of robbing emigrants bound for the lands across the Appalachians. At least five murders were laid at their door before they were caught and imprisoned at Danville, Kentucky, but before they could be brought to trial they broke out of their flimsy jail and vanished. Within weeks the word got around that the brothers were robbing and murdering along the perilous Wilderness Road from Virginia to Kentucky.

The full story of their butcheries will probably never be known, but it is on record that many of their victims were disembowelled, mutilated, or otherwise horribly tortured before being killed. Finally, even their grim companions spurned them and drove them away, describing them as wolves, not men.

In appearance the brothers were typical frontiersmen. Their hair and beards were jet black and unkempt, and both were dressed in buckskins. Each carried a musket, tomahawk, pig-sticking knife and powder flask. For more than a year after their jail-break they meandered through the forests of Kentucky, killing game or men as the mood possessed them. Like so many dangerous characters, they had a gentler side and a macabre sense of humour. Years later, one old-timer recalled offering two men hospitality, and when they left him they gave him a powder flask to 'help protect you from the terrible Harpes'. Only later did he learn who they were and how lucky he had been.

Finally, in 1799, the brothers were cornered. Wiley escaped, but Big Harpe was shot in the spine. The posse that had tracked him down gathered around waiting for him to die, but he took his time. Impatiently, one of the group took a knife and started to saw through the dying monster's neck. Angrily, Big Harpe roared: 'You are a God damned rough butcher, but cut on and be damned!' So the man finished cutting and took off his head as he might have a hog's.

During the journey home the posse ran out of food and, so the legend goes, turned to cannibalism. Harpe's head was boiled in a pot of corn and later nailed to a tree. They named the tree Harpe's Head, and for years afterwards his gleaming white skull grinned down at startled strangers.

Five years after Big Harpe's death, a villain named Sam Mason was killed by a man named Setten, who had offered to bring him in. Setten returned with Mason's head in a ball of clay, but interest in the head rapidly diminished when someone in the crowd recognised Setten as Wiley Harpe. He was quickly arrested, tried and hanged on 8 February 1804, and with his death the Harpes reign of terror was at an end.

11
Vigilante justice in Texas in 1881, drawn for the benefit of readers of Frank Leslie's Illustrated Newspaper.

some cowboys in Arizona had been shooting at each other early in the morning to 'increase the circulation of the blood', but were forced to stop when one of them was shot in the foot. Childish and irresponsible such actions may have been, but they did bring temporary relief from the tension and boredom that were so much part of Frontier life.

But it was the tension that dominated. When the Kansas Territory was opened up to settlement in the early 1850s there was no lack of immigrants; but with them came an ugly fact of life – slavery. Those who wished to create a new land free of human bondage were violently opposed by those equally determined to keep it. The result was war and bloodshed. Kansas 'Free-soilers' fought openly with the 'Border Ruffians' from Missouri. Writing home to his mother, James Butler Hickok, newly arrived in the territory and not yet called Wild Bill, noted:

You don't know what a country this is for drinking and fighting, but I hope it will be different some time, and I know in reason that it will when the Law is put in force. There is no Common Law here hardly at all. A man can do what he pleases without fear of the Law or anything else. There have been two

12
A sketch that says it all. Vigilantes returning from the scene of a hanging in the mid 1860s.

awful fights in town this week, you don't know anything about such fighting at home as I speak of, this is no place for women and children yet, although they say it is so quiet here . . . if a man fights in Kansas and gets whipped he never say anything more about it, if he does he will get whipped for his trouble.

Abolitionists like the fiery fanatic, John Brown, whose religious beliefs were Old Testament at its toughest, and who left death and destruction in his wake, were matched with equal savagery by the pro-slavery supporters. John Brown's activities came to a sudden end when he was captured following an abortive raid on the Harper's Ferry Arsenal, and he was hanged in December 1859. But the violence in Kansas continued well into the Civil War.

The West was not alone in the violence stakes, for the East and South, too, still suffered from outbreaks of it. The city of New York spawned innumerable criminals and, if contemporary accounts are to be believed, some of its inhabitants were as bad or worse than the so-called 'Bad Men' of the West. Many who moved westwards carried lawlessness with them or were those to whom killing and robbing had become a way of life. Guns, the symbol of authority or power rapidly became the accepted tools of survival. Those who maintain that guns do not kill, only the men behind them, oversimplify the situation. And there are times when only the gun can save society from the bully and the coward.

It was because the West was a largely unknown region and consequently not governed by state or Federal laws that led every man to be armed with a weapon of some sort. And the further west they went so it was harder for what law there was to offer protection. States on the eastern seaboard and down as far as Louisiana tried many methods of curtailing the use of arms. The carrying of weapons was made illegal, but it was almost impossible to enforce. Southern tradition – particularly in Texas, where in the middle 1850s almost every man and boy owned or carried a pistol of some sort – demanded that each man should be able to defend himself and

13
Holding down a lot in Guthrie, a town in what is now Oklahoma that sprang from a population of nought to 10,000 in a single wild day in 1889, when yet more Indian land was opened to the whites.

14
A common scene in Hays City, Kansas. On 6 September 1873, David Roberts shot and killed Peter Welsh and George H. Summer, both soldiers, in front of Cy Goddard's saloon.

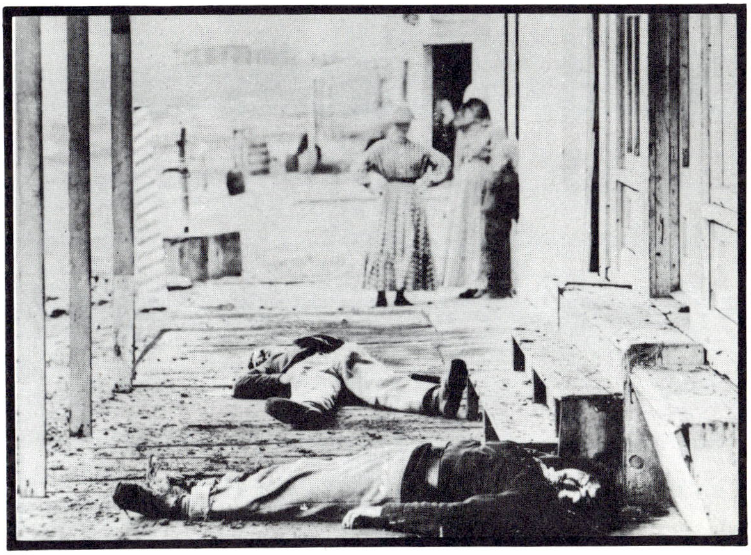

his honour. As with the Regency Bucks in England, and the French even later, the most ridiculous slights prompted duels or shoot-outs that today are difficult to understand. But they were deadly serious at the time, and, as we shall see, many of the shoot-outs in the cowtowns and mining camps were equally incomprehensible.

It is strange that as the frontier West became more populated and so-called civilisation crept closer, so violence and sudden death increased. Some people argued that civilisation brought with it established restrictions and that the free-thinking attitude of pioneers hindered rather than furthered progress. Nevertheless, there were other more obvious reasons. One was simple. Gold, at first the shared secret of a few, rapidly attracted such a vast number of would-be miners that the men had to be prepared to fight, and kill, to protect what they believed was rightly theirs. Another reason was the potential wealth of the cattle industry, already thriving before the Civil War, but booming to unprecedented heights following the war. It proved to be the saviour of the defeated South. All manner of men, some familiar with cattle and others only interested in quick profits, descended upon the brush country of Texas and soon vast herds of longhorn cattle began pushing their way north to Missouri and Kansas to meet up with the railroads. The great cattle ranches in Texas were emulated in Montana, Wyoming and Arizona, and again there was conflict.

As more and more men grew rich from cattle and gold-mining, and news of their profits spread, so too did more and more people push westwards anxious to get their share of the spoils. But the latecomers were soon made to realise that what they did get they would have to fight for. Some took up farming and with government approval took over several acres of prairie land and set about the job of cultivation in a quiet but determined manner. Others, however, were more daring (or foolish) and fenced off sections of what had formerly been open range, owned by no one but 'claimed' by the cattlemen because they had been there first and felt no need to stake their claims. These 'nesters', as the cattlemen called them, became the targets for much abuse and in some cases violence.

So it was that despite the onward surge of civilisation, the establishment of law and order and a concerted effort by those in authority to curtail violence, the Frontier was far from safe. But as we shall see, before there could be any hope of establishing law and order, the West and its people had to overcome greed and violence; and one of the most destructive features of the battle over who owned what and why, was the range feuds and wars that for thirty years helped retard the taming of the frontier West.

EARLY FIREARMS

As more and more people pushed westwards, the need for firearms increased. Would-be explorers and settlers needed guns to protect themselves from attacks by hostile Indians and wild animals or to shoot game in order to survive.

By the mid-1780s the majority of weapons were still smooth bore, but a number of rifled arms were in use, notably the German Jaeger rifles. These huge, heavy single-shot weapons when properly loaded were extremely accurate. But from a military point of view the smooth-bore musket was a far more practical proposition, for the simplicity of its flintlock ignition, comparative ease of loading and massed firepower, made it the ideal weapon for the average soldier, whose lack of education and largely undeveloped intelligence balked at some of the more complicated arms.

The loading procedure was quite simple. A measured charge of black powder from a flask or animal horn was poured down the barrel, and a lead ball was then rammed down on top of it. The pan of the lock was also primed with gunpowder, the cover closed and the hammer, which contained the flint, was cocked and the gun was ready for action. When the trigger was pulled the flint struck the pan cover or frizzen and the sparks were deflected into the pan, setting off the powder which in turn flashed through a hole into the barrel and ignited the powder in the barrel and discharged the ball. Loading was slow, so most frontiersmen learned not to waste ammunition, and the majority of them became good shots.

In England in the 1770s, where the Brown Bess musket had been the standard military arm for almost 200 years, another arm appeared. This was the breech-loading rifle invented by Captain Patrick Ferguson. Although his design owed something to the Frenchman Isaac de la Chaumette, his improvements made it an extremely practical weapon.

Ferguson demonstrated his rifle at Woolwich before experts (in pouring rain and high winds) and was able to hit a target 200 yards away six times a minute. He then started to walk towards the target firing and loading as he did so, and got off four shots a minute! Unfortunately, his death at the battle of King's Mountain in October 1780, and conservatism in high places, meant the end of his remarkable weapon, and the British continued to use the Brown Bess.

In the United States, however, German immigrant gunsmiths who had settled in Pennsylvania took as their basic idea the Jaeger and produced a much lighter, long-barrelled small-calibred rifled arm which today is known as the Kentucky rifle. These weapons, though slow to load, were deadly accurate and when used by experts (against man or beast) could kill at several hundred yards' range.

Pistols, too, were available in unlimited numbers, so the frontiersmen who set out to explore or settle the early West were well armed and able to defend themselves against most man-made or natural hazards.

VIGILANTE HUMOUR

Once during a particularly hectic spell of violence in one of the mining camps, the Vigilante Committee found that they had a full programme. It happened that a prospective candidate for hemp justice had doubt on his side, so the jury took longer than usual in deliberating their verdict. After about half an hour there came a knock on the door and the leader of the Committee put his head around it and enquired if they had reached a verdict.

'No, we ain't,' snapped back the foreman impatiently.

'Okay, gents, take your time, only remember we're awaitin' fer the room to lay out the corpse!'

On another occasion following a hanging, someone suggested that they tell the man's widow. After some deliberation they picked upon the most likely man to do it – on account of his tactfulness – and he walked down to her shack. Knocking on the door he asked her if the 'widow Jones' was at home.

'I'm Mrs Jones – I'm not a widow.'

'Do you want to bet on that?'

Perhaps one of the most macabre incidents of rope justice was an event that took place in Benton, Montana, in August 1868. As Bill Hynson was standing outside the post office a man stopped beside him. 'Say, Bill, we need your help. A man's goin' to be jerked off on the orders of the Vigilance Committee, and we need a good strong rope and scaffold.'

'I'm game,' Bill grinned evilly, only too anxious to witness some unfortunate's end.

'Right then, follow me.' Bill eagerly questioned his companion as to the name of the man and his crime, but was told that he would know soon enough. Between them they had soon erected a good strong scaffold and Bill and his companion stood side by side as members of the Committee approached and stood in a group around it. Suddenly, the leader jumped onto the scaffold and, with Bill's companion, pinioned Hynson's arms to his side and adjusted the rope around his neck.

'Hey!' gasped Bill, 'what you fellows think you're doin'?'

'We've reached our verdict, Bill, and that is you will be hanged by the neck until you're good and dead for the murder of a Chinee-woman, the stealin' of a rifle and robbery!'

Hynson's reply was lost in a choking gurgle as he slipped into the air from a platform he helped to construct!

2 FEUDING AND FIGHTING

Reports from Lincoln County indicate a renewal of hostilities between adverse factions; both parties are in the field and a collision is imminent. If they should succeed in completely destroying each other the result would be hailed by all good citizens.

Las Vegas *Gazette*, 22 June 1878

Feuding has been 'as American as apple pie' for more than a century, but in the old days any kind of feud was taken very seriously. What might have started off as a minor dispute between individuals sometimes spread alarmingly. The result was often multiple death and disaster.

Cattle was a major source of trouble. The most famous of all range wars was mainly caused by disputes over cattle and the economic power that they bought. In Lincoln County, New Mexico, during the late 1870s and early 1880s a veritable state of war existed; one of the minor participants being William McCarty, alias Bonney – Billy the Kid – who became a legend.

Billy's most notorious exploits, (see Chapter 3) came after the famous, desperate conflict was virtually over. The Lincoln County war was not so much a range war as a lethal struggle for the economic and political control of an area in south-east New Mexico which then consisted of a quarter of the entire territory.

This sparsely populated land, not yet completely wrested from the Apaches, held an explosive mixture of Indians, Mexicans and Americans. The county seat was a Mexican settlement which had become Lincoln, and several miles away was Fort Stanton, built in 1855 – a very active post well into the 1880s.

The seeds of the feud were sown in the early 1870s, when three Irishmen and a German took control of the county so completely that writers of books and screenplays have been blessing them ever since. The original partners were two Civil War veterans, Laurence G. Murphy and Emil Fritz, who were later joined by two younger men, James J. Dolan and John H. Riley. These four ran Lincoln's main store, the House. They also ran cattle on the ranges and might be said to have run the county sheriff, another Irishman named William Brady. Best of all they held contracts to supply beef to both the Mescalero Apache Reservation and Fort Stanton, the key to their fortunes, which were improved still more because they were linked with an unsavoury group of businessmen and politicians known as the Santa Fe Ring. By the time war broke out in 1878, Fritz was dead and Murphy was a sick man in virtual retirement, leaving the field to their two ruthless young colleagues, especially Dolan.

Murphy and his friends were hated and feared by the smalltimers of Lincoln County who were forced to buy their overpriced goods, forced to accept low prices for cattle, and could never feel secure in their properties. Meanwhile, this New Mexican mafia swindled the Indians out of their proper rations and kept on good terms with the authorities in Fort Stanton. All the while lawlessness ranging from cattle-rustling to killings was rampant in Lincoln County.

By 1877, the Murphy empire was being seriously threatened by an ambitious trio, ruthless in their different ways, but infinitely more attractive and considerably more reputable than their corrupt and power-drunk opponents. One was the Cattle King, John Chisum, who ruled a ranchland kingdom along the Pecos River like a benevolent despot. He suspected that Murphy men were running off his cattle, and wanted the House's lucrative beef contracts. He befriended a young Canadian of Scots parentage, Alexander McSween, who had been a lawyer in Kansas before coming to Lincoln with his wife. McSween, who had political ambitions, was the area's only lawyer and like Chisum he never carried a gun.

15
John H. Tunstall, the young English rancher whose murder triggered off the Lincoln County war. One of his employees was destined to become a legend – Billy the Kid.

16 and 17
Alexander McSween, Tunstall's colleague, believed in the law, but he perished by the gun. His tragic, heroic widow Sue survived the nightmare in Lincoln County to become a rancher in her own right, dying in 1931.

In 1876, an Englishman arrived on the scene. He was John Tunstall, the son of a rich London merchant. Born in Dalston, London, in 1853, Tunstall came to Lincoln after stays in Canada and California. He had a charming personality, boundless big business hopes, and an English belief in the rule of law. With his father's help, and with Chisum lending both money and a famous name, Tunstall, then partnered by McSween, opened a store-cum-bank a mere quarter of a mile from Murphy's store. He wrote to his father that his intention was to control Lincoln County and take 50 cents of every dollar spent in it.

He and McSween were soon taking trade from the House, the majority of the locals welcoming them because they offered a fair deal – and were not like Murphy, Dolan or Riley. McSween had already fallen out with the Irishmen because of legal wrangles over Emil Fritz's will, which had resulted in false accusations being hurled at the lawyer, whom they had employed as the only one available. Now, with trade going to the newcomers, and with local newspapers carrying vituperative letters from the rival parties, tension rapidly mounted, exacerbated because McSween refused to hand over much-needed insurance money to the irate Dolan and Riley. Gunsmoke was inevitable, especially after Dolan managed to have McSween arrested for alleged embezzlement and, for a time, even the great John Chisum for alleged debts.

The Tunstall - McSween - Chisum faction had the little people of Lincoln County to back them, and a handful of tough young men. These included Tunstall's foreman, Richard 'Dick' Brewer, who also had a small ranch of his own, and Billy the Kid, to whom Tunstall had taken a liking. He had arrived under a cloud, as we shall see, but in fact had by Frontier standards a very un-criminal past, whatever the legends suggest.

Dolan and Murphy, for all their current shortage of cash, were considerably more powerful, not only for the reasons already given, but because they had small armies of rustlers and worse in their pay.

The law, as administered by Dolan and Riley's creature, Sheriff Brady, now followed up a writ of attachment on McSween's property with one on all the property in the J. H. Tunstall & Co store. Tension rapidly built up and the climax came on 18 February 1878 when Tunstall set out for Lincoln from his ranch, driving six horses excluded from the writ of attachment by an agreement with Brady. With the Englishman rode Dick Brewer, Billy the Kid, John Middleton, and Robert Widenmann, little knowing that a large posse, led by Brady's deputy Mathews, was after them. It contained known criminals and jail-breakers.

Widenmann and Brewer were the first to scent danger. They had ridden ahead looking for wild turkeys, when they glanced back and saw a small body of men bearing down on Tunstall. The rest of the posse was some distance behind. The pair shouted at their three friends and Billy and Middleton galloped to them, thinking Tunstall was with them, as a fusillade of bullets cut through the air around them. They reached some boulders and took cover.

John Tunstall, meanwhile, had turned and, out of sight of his men, awaited the riders. Three men appeared out of the trees that screened the ensuing tragedy from Tunstall's men. They were William S. Morton, Brady's deputy, Jessie [*sic*] Evans, a vicious bandit leader recently sprung from jail, and Tom Hill, also wanted by the law.

The trio wasted no time. It was probably Morton who rode up to Tunstall and shot him out of his saddle, after which Evans grabbed the dead Englishman's pistol and fired into his body, killing his horse as the rest of the men came into sight. The posse was told by Morton that Tunstall had opened fire.

The four sheltering behind the rocks had no doubt what had happened, though it was Middleton who voiced their thoughts: 'They have killed Tunstall!' Only the foolish have ever blamed them for not riding to his rescue, for as they were outnumbered by at least four to one, such a gesture would have been hopeless. Instead, they headed for Lincoln, followed by the killers who proclaimed that Tunstall had died 'resisting arrest'. His death triggered off the Lincoln County war and caused a minor international incident, for Tunstall senior filed claims for compensation which were finally refuted in 1885, three years after the old man had died.

Whether or not Billy the Kid stood over the grave of his employer and said: 'Tunstall was the only man that ever treated me decent. I'll kill the men who did this to him!' is open to conjecture, but the speech has an element of poetic truth. Nevertheless, Dick Brewer and the Kid with other Tunstall men were soon seeking revenge. Armed with warrants issued by a friendly JP, eleven 'Regulators' led by Brewer captured Morton, Tunstall's probable murderer, and Frank Baker, both of whom were killed on the way back to Lincoln, 'resisting arrest'. So was one of the posse, William McCloskey, who had, it is said, sworn to protect the pair. The circumstances were confused, but not the implication, 'an eye for an eye'.

The atmosphere both in Lincoln County and the town was electric, not least because the Dolan faction's war cry was: 'Tunstall is gone. We must get McSween next!' But it was McSween's side who struck first, for on 1 April, Sheriff Brady and his deputies, Mathews, 'Dad' Peppin and Hindman, were ambushed from behind a wall beside Tunstall's store in Lincoln. Brady was killed and Hindman mortally wounded. One of the killers was Billy the Kid, who was slightly wounded in the thigh when running for a fallen Winchester. Meanwhile, though not as part of the war, two of the posse that killed Tunstall, Jessie Evans and Tom Hill, after their brief service with the 'law', returned to banditry and tried to rob a sheepherder's camp. Hill was killed and Evans retired wounded, heading for treatment at Fort Stanton, where the authorities were scandalously to favour the House throughout the war.

On 4 April, Dick Brewer, the Kid and eleven others ambushed and finally killed another of the posse that killed Tunstall, but their victim, tough, crippled Andrew 'Buckshot' Roberts, killed Brewer and so conducted himself that the 'Gunfight at Blazer's Mill' is given the treatment its epic quality deserves in Chapter 9.

Of the score or more who died directly or indirectly as a result of the war, the most famous victim was McSween, who was killed at the climax of a five day pitched battle in July in Lincoln itself. On the 14th some forty or fifty McSween men rode in to repossess and hold the town, which had become Dolan territory. The new sheriff, George 'Dad' Peppin, was taken by surprise, most of his men being out of town watching another spot, and the McSween forces established themselves in three buildings, the pick of them, gunfighters both American and Mexican, being with the lawyer in his own house. The redoubtable Mrs McSween, who later became a ranch-woman and lived until 1931, insisted on staying with her husband. Meanwhile, Peppin's men returned to town, roughly equal in numbers to the McSweens, and positioned themselves strategically enough for them to be besieging their enemies.

For three days, despite an enormous wastage of ammunition, casualties were limited to a horse, a mule and one of Peppin's men who was badly wounded, while the Dolan men were hoping for intervention on the side of 'law and order' by Colonel Dudley at Fort Stanton. New regulations prevented the Colonel moving troops in as yet, as he longed to do, so Dolan went up to the fort to get him to change his mind. He succeeded, and Dudley decided to place troops in Lincoln 'for the preservation of the lives of the women and children, and in response to numerous petitions received from persons in that town'. So just as the McSween faction felt that they were winning, they were confronted, on Friday 19 July, with a Gatling gun, a mountain howitzer, thirty men and every officer from the fort except one. It would be straining the truth in view of what happened that day to suggest that the force was neutral!

Dudley was invincibly ignorant rather than criminally in the pocket of Dolan. Totally biassed against McSween, he allowed a warrant to be made out against him with his signature on it, while the sight of his troops so alarmed the largest group of McSween men that they left their buildings, the Montano House, and fled. Most of them were Mexicans, but three, Bowdre, Scurlock and Middleton, were hard core Tunstall fighters.

Events now turned desperate for the McSweens. Colonel Dudley spurned McSween's attempts to question his actions, and the lawyer seems to have asked without success to surrender not to Peppin but the military. When his enemies had already set fire to his house to drive him and his men out, his brave wife went to plead with Dudley, whose blinkered mind was so rigidly pro-Dolan that he treated her abominably. So she returned to the slowly burning building. On both journeys she risked assassination, for her frank speaking made it uncertain that the Dolans would obey the unwritten law that women should not be harmed.

A conference was held, with Billy the Kid coming to the fore as leader, for McSween had become depressed to the point of not caring what happened. The Kid advised a break to the river and asked Mrs McSween to leave before them as 'a dress ain't very good to make a run in'. Reluctantly she agreed.

That night, when the fire had almost consumed the house down to the last room, Billy and two of his men made the first break. One of them, Harvey Morris, died instantly, the others sprinted safely to the river, unharmed by random firing. McSween and the rest left their escape longer than Billy had advised and paid the penalty. Their offer to surrender did them no good, five being shot down, including the unarmed McSween. His wife later related how he had fallen on his knees and called: 'I surrender. Oh, my God save me. Oh, Lord, Lord save me!' But they shot him down like a dog and tore up burning boards and piled them on his body. Throughout the war his courage had never failed him, but at the end he seemed to have lost his will to live. Later a judge was to sum up the two sides: 'Both have done many things contrary to law. McSween I firmly believe, acted conscientiously; Murphy and Co, for private gain and revenge.'

Officially that was the end of the war and the moment that Billy the Kid turned to crime. The drama of those final days and their nightmare quality is best summed up by the events of the 21st when Mrs McSween was searching the ruins of her home. One Andy Boyle laughed at her efforts to save a carpet and said: 'By God, we've killed McSween and we'll get you next.'

'Well, kill me,' retorted the amazing woman. 'You have already taken away all that was precious to me, my husband and my home. I'd just as soon you'd take my life.' Finally, her courage shamed her tormentors and they left her to make a new life.

Unhappily, the chief villain of this saga, Dolan, survived to become a power in New Mexican politics, even though J. J. Dolan & Co was lost to him by mortgage foreclosure. Both Tunstall's properties became his, proving yet again that crime pays. It did his partner no harm either. As for John Chisum, he had taken no direct part in the war; he will enter this story again in connection with Billy the Kid. Let us leave him and this greatest of Western

18
When homesteaders and others decided to fence their meagre acres there was often trouble, with irate cattlemen hiring men to cut the wires, or worse. Sometimes they did it openly, sometimes, as here – in Nebraska – suitably disguised.

feuds hoping that it is true that he gave Sue McSween a gift of a small herd of cattle. Certainly this magnificent woman became a successful rancher.

Arizona, long noted for its strife, was the scene of a conflict equally as bloody as the Lincoln County fracas, for here in the 1880s the Grahams and the Tewksburys fought the now legendary sheep war that inspired Zane Grey's famous novel, *To the Last Man*.

Details of this ferocious feud are too involved to summarise, but the outlines are simple enough. It happened in central Arizona's Tonto Basin, called, ironically, Pleasant Valley in the 1880s by the few cowmen who lived in the lonely area seventy miles from the nearest white settlement.

Into the valley in 1880 had come Boston-born John D. Tewksbury, his second wife, and his grown half-Indian sons, John Junior, Edwin and James, and two years later Thomas H. Graham and his brother John arrived. They were joined two years latei by their younger half-brother William. The Tewksbury boys and the Grahams occasionally worked for local ranches and seem to have stolen stock from one of them, James Stinson's, then fallen out over the loot.

From this small-scale beginning a feud developed. Partisans joined the Grahams, then the Tewksburys threatened to bring sheep onto the range, the ultimate crime. Until the early years of this century, cattlemen looked on sheep with loathing, believing that they devoured and therefore destroyed the grass, and fouled waterholes and streams. Mutton never crossed their lips, in fact to eat sheep was considered degenerate, and the wretched 'woolies' were murdered by the thousand, along with scores of hated sheepmen, before the latter won the right to stay and even ranchers found that they could raise both animals.

That was long after the slaughter in Pleasant Valley. The line beyond which sheep were forbidden was the rim of the Mogollon Mountains, which towered over the north of the valley, but one electric day in 1886, as the cowboy turned author Earle R. Forrest related in his classic *Arizona's Dark and Bloody Ground* (1936), the cry was passed from man to man, from ranch to ranch: 'The Tewksburys are driving sheep over the rim of the Mogollons!'

The war that followed lasted until 1892, by which time at least seventeen had died violently, three had been lynched, and probably eight more had been killed. All three Grahams died of lead-poisoning, along with John Tewksbury Jr, and no one, not even neutrals, could avoid being threatened or worse by the war. One of them, Frederick R. Burnham, who later became a soldier of fortune as a Western peace officer and a scout during the Matabele, Zulu and Boer Wars, wrote in his autobiography, *Scouting on Two Continents* (1926), about the feud:

> Even the little children absorbed the fear around them and showed pathetic furtiveness. I recall a day when three of us, all heavily armed, rode up to a cabin on Tonto Creek and saw a little girl, about five years old, carrying a white pitcher of water from the spring to the house. When the child sighted us, she gave a scream, dropped the pitcher, and ran – not to the house, as a child ordinarily would, but to the creek bottom, shouting at the top of her voice: 'Daddy! Here they come to kill you.' She already understood that her own presence in the cabin might deter her father from shooting the enemy. Fortunately Daddy was not an impulsive man and was not disposed to fire until quite satisfied it was against a foe. But the little girl refused to come out of hiding until her mother's voice called, with just the right ring of assurance.

The most famous single event of the feud was only indirectly concerned with it, and was a gunfight – between Sheriff Commodore Perry Owens and a houseful of killers – so extraordinary that it is featured solo in Chapter 9. But the most haunting incident was very much part of the feud proper, a scene of stark tragedy, and a reminder, like the saga of Mrs McSween in Lincoln County, of just how much the women of the West were involved when the firing started.

When the war was reaching its height soon after William Graham was gunned down by James D. Houck, a sheepman with a deputy's badge who was a Tewksbury partisan, Tom and John Graham gathered their supporters and headed for the Tewksbury cabin. As they laid siege to it, they caught John Tewksbury Jr and a friend outside the cabin and left them dead and in full view of those inside.

The gun battle that followed went on for hours, until suddenly hogs appeared that began to devour the two bodies in front of the cabin. But the besiegers neither granted a truce for burials nor drove the beasts away with bullets, and the hogs, as Forrest puts it, 'grunted contentedly over their ghastly feast', as bullets went on thudding into the log walls of the cabin.

Suddenly a scream rang out. It was John Tewksbury's widow who shrieked: 'I can't stand it. I must bury them. They'll have to kill me to stop me.' She flung open the door and appeared with a shovel, marching purposefully towards the corpses. The hail of bullets continued, then died away in shame. As she dug two shallow graves, silence reigned, broken only by the wailing of her infant child in the cabin. Then she walked back, went in, and the shooting started again, only ending when a justice of the peace arrived with a posse, causing the besiegers to flee.

Another woman, this time a Graham, was to provide an equally dramatic, if less horrific, moment. In 1892, when it seemed that the feud had died down, Tom Graham, the last of the brothers, was murdered, and Ed Tewksbury and one of his closest supporters, John Rhodes, were arrested on strong circumstantial evidence. At a hearing before a justice of the peace, Tom Graham's brave twenty - two - year - old widow drew his six-shooter from her umbrella, pressed its muzzle against Rhodes' back and squeezed the trigger. It failed to go off and before Mrs Graham could act again, pandemonium broke out and she was hurried out of court by friends. To the fury of many, Rhodes was discharged, later marrying none other than the widow of John Tewksbury.

These accounts of Frontier violence have emphasised only too clearly the involvement of lawless men either personally or as partisans in the numerous family and community feuds that split the West. Easterners, who even now are inclined to view the shoot-outs between feuding families with amusement, cannot be blamed for assuming that the West, too, looked with benign tolerance upon their own outbursts. But they did not: out West it was always a very serious matter.

It is perhaps not surprising that some of the most famous Western feuds took place in Texas where even today descendants of the original participants do not take kindly to questions from prying outsiders. One good reason for Texas feuding was the state of law and order then prevailing. Texas remained a Frontier community for much longer than most other States, and despite the activities of the Rangers in combating lawlessness, people still believed they knew best how to take care of their own problems.

Texans were a very mixed crowd. Many of them came originally from the Southern States and brought with them a code of honour which dictated that every man was expected to right his own wrongs or those of his nearest and dearest whatever religion or the law might demand. Add to that the Frontier 'Code' – which was a more basic approach than the Southern variety – and you had all the ingredients for trouble. The Code according to Texans was an up-dated version of 'an eye for an eye' which often meant 'shoot first and ask questions later' but was intended to imply that 'honour' was placed above all.

It did not help either that because of its vastness, its lack of civilisation and its acknowledged lawlessness, every wanted man (and some women) fled there when the going got too hot. Other Western states soon accepted that wanted individuals had escaped to Texas, and they even coined the emigrants' name for it – GTT: Gone to Texas.

With so much land and so few people, corrupt, persuasive men could raise a band of followers who, for a price, would use guns. By the 1850s and well into the early 1870s, a staggering amount of corruption and villainy was practised. With it came killings and in the wake of the killings came the feuds.

One writer in the early 1850s noted that every male of walking age in Texas carried a pistol, and this was not too much of an exaggeration. School children were reputed to be armed, and it was not unknown for their teachers to keep, besides the conventional cane, a pistol in their desks. Even preachers were said to enter the pulpit armed with 'prayerbook and pistol'.

The outlawry that infested Texas in the early 1840s soon resulted in disagreement between rival factions and the so-called vigilantes who sprang up in equal numbers. Although their actions in certain areas, particularly California where they had decisively curbed the outlaw element, were often a boon and a necessity, the vigilantes in Texas were all too often nothing more than cut-throat gangs preying upon each other and those who opposed them.

Unscrupulous men on the make were quite prepared to use vigilance organisations to hurry things up a little. This was particularly true of the 'Regulators' and the 'Moderators' whose actions set the pattern for most of the feuds which followed, for the typical Texas feud followed two courses, a 'Moderator' or 'mob' vendetta or the family quarrel.

The Moderators originated in 1840 following the killing of a man named Goodbread by a certain Charles W. Jackson. Apparently, Jackson had been told by one Alfred George, a prospective candidate for sheriff of Shelby County, Texas, that Goodbread intended to kill Jackson on sight. Angered and afraid, Jackson sought out the unfortunate Goodbread and shot him, unaware that he had been used by George as a means of getting rid of a potential rival. The upshot was that Goodbread's death sparked off the war between the Regulators and the Moderators.

Within months the state was in uproar. Friends of Goodbread set out to kill Jackson, and with the help of his new-found friend George, now the sheriff, Jackson was able to avoid coming to trial for the murder of Goodbread. Soon Jackson's Regulators (originally called the 'Shelby Guards') were engaged in a reign of terror that forced the friends of Goodbread to form their own gang – the 'Moderators', who killed Jackson from ambush. The fighting continued, and it was only the personal intervention of President Sam Houston, backed by four companies of militia, that brought the fighting to a close.

But it was not always so simple. Far more serious were the feuds between families, and it was these that even today cause friction and sometimes actual bodily harm to the unwary and prying stranger.

Among the more noted family feuds was that between the Suttons and the Taylors. This is remembered chiefly because one of the participants on the Taylor side was John Wesley Hardin, one of the West's most notorious killers.

The trouble began soon after the Civil War ended. DeWitt County, situated halfway between San Antonio and the Gulf Coast, a largely cattle-raising region, also produced cotton. And it was fear of trouble with the blacks that first caused violence to erupt. As the Civil War came to an end, and the defeated South tried to take stock of what was left to it, the freed slaves also took a long, hard look at their own plight. Few of them had jobs, and those that were prepared to work demanded so much that they priced themselves out of work. In retaliation the whites accused some of them of horse-stealing, drunkenness, carrying weapons and and of insulting their former masters. Yankee soldiers, too, were a problem, for they had a distressing habit of disarming anyone no matter what his business. Crops failed and the general political situation as it then existed left many people convinced that emigration was the answer. Youngsters, however, seemed to be more practical, although many of them wanted to leave school as soon as possible to become cowboys or stock branders. And sometimes they were not too careful where the cattle came from.

Rustling in Texas had reached new heights during the late 1860s and the sons of one Creed Taylor were soon wanted by the military. The youngsters were joined by others and the 'Taylor Gang' became wanted men. In 1868 a sheriff's posse got on the gang's trail, and one of the posse members, Bill Sutton, was stated by the press to be responsible for the killing of a member of the gang, Charles Taylor, in the town of Bastrop. It was reported that the gang had stolen stock in Clinton and that this included a horse with a fine silver-mounted saddle. After Taylor's death the animal was recovered and Sutton boasted of his exploit and, according to the legend, sparked off the Sutton-Taylor feud.

It was a bad business. Men were dragged from their beds and shot, others were hanged and a number of homesteads burned down. By 1873, when the violence was at its height, the Taylor faction was joined by John Wesley Hardin whose cousin, Jeff Hardin, had married Creed Taylor's daughter Mary. During his brief period as a gang member, Wes led a number of daring raids against the Suttons and is alleged to have shot some of the men who, tradition asserts, helped make up the alleged 'forty notches' on his gun. But Wes did not stay with the gang very long for he was himself running out of places to hide. Thanks to the efforts of the Texas Rangers both factions were slowly whittled down and each side was also actively engaged in decimating the other, so that by 1877, with the death of Jim Taylor, the feud was virtually over.

No discussion of Western feuds or range wars would be complete without mention of the Johnson County Cattle war of 1892, for this classic encounter has long served as the basis for innumerable plots in Western movies and books, and represents all that was bad in politics and the conflicts between cattlemen and 'nesters'.

If the Lincoln County war was a struggle for power that became a tragic epic, and the Pleasant Valley war a particularly lethal example of feudin', fightin' families, the Johnson County war was a classic compound of villainy, ruthlessness and stark heroism. It has inspired a literary and cinematic masterpiece, Jack Schaffer's *Shane*, and in its own time it triggered off a searing polemic by the writer and publisher, A. S. Mercer, who was lucky to get out of Wyoming alive. Until the University of Oklahoma Press republished his book *The Banditti of the Plains* in 1954, it was virtually unobtainable, so eager were his enemies to suppress it: even the Library of Congress 'lost' its copyright copies. Mercer subtitled his book 'The Cattlemen's Invasion of Wyoming in 1892', then, as if that was not strong enough, gave it another subtitle in brackets and capitals: (THE CROWNING INFAMY OF THE AGES).

Back in the 1870s and the 1880s Wyoming's first ranchers had made fortunes on the open range, becoming cattle barons of the territory, and some had risen that much faster by branding strays and rustling, the very crimes of which they were later to accuse their enemies. Meanwhile, farmers and small ranchers had been entering the territory in growing numbers to take up the free land offered under the Homestead Act of 1862.

Then disaster struck the range. Overstocking and drought and a slump in the price of beef in 1886 were followed by the worst winter in Western history, which may have killed as many as three quarters of Wyoming's cattle. Those ranchers who survived the holocaust began to use more modern methods and started growing hay for winter food. The market gradually improved as herds were built up once more on ranges that would never again be overstocked. But the steady stream of settlers continued to squat on the open range of Wyoming, which became a state in 1890.

Tension between the two sides mounted swiftly, until cattle barons came to regard all the 'intruders' as rustlers, which some of them undoubtedly were. But little evidence suggests that the majority were anything more than hard-working small-timers trying to make a living.

19 and 20
The lynching of Jim Averill and Ella Watson by cattle baron Albert Bothwell and friends was the prelude to the Johnson County war. No one was ever prosecuted for the outrages, which stir up controversy to this day.

Their opponents were not corrupt – until they took drastic and murderous action – in the way that the Murphy-Dolan-Santa Fe Gang in New Mexico were, but they resented the homesteaders on principle and had the power to make their resentment felt. The Wyoming Stock Growers' Association, some 100 strong, had the state governor and its senators on its roster, its most notable coup being the 'maverick law' which allowed every unbranded calf found on the range to become its property. Its members claimed that the law was directed against rustlers, and sold the strays by auction at prices usually too high for smaller cattlemen to buy back their strays.

The money obtained in this way paid the wages of the cattle barons' hired detectives, who received $250 for convicting a rustler. As the chief of the Association's detectives was an unsavoury Texan gunslinger named Frank Canton, ordinary Wyoming folk loathed and feared them and their bosses.

Their fears were based on a series of violent incidents, the most notorious of which happened south of Johnson County on the Sweetwater range. There, two homesteaders, James Averill and Ella Watson, had settled as neighbours on the river, Averill run-

ning a store and a saloon and post office, and Ella, a Canadian, exchanging her favours with the local cowboys for cattle, some of which were probably stolen. They were on land claimed by the cattle baron, Albert Bothwell, and Averill, a justice of the peace, made himself even more unpopular by writing in the Casper *Weekly Mail* of 7 April 1889 that the cattlemen were speculators and land grabbers.

That July, Bothwell and some friends appeared at their cabins and, without the semblance of a trial, hanged them both on the same tree. Later, when there was an outcry, Ella was turned by judicious propaganda into 'Cattle Kate', the rustler, who had to die, according to one apologist, 'for the good of the country'. No one was prosecuted, and nor was anyone for the lynching of a homesteader named Waggoner, called from his home by three men, one of whom claimed to be a deputy US marshal. Eight days later, he was found hanging from a tree some miles away.

Waggoner died in June 1891, and that November, assassins crept up on the cabin of W. H. Hall on the Powder, who was away. While two remained outside, two more broke in and saw Hall's room-mates, Ross Gilbertson and Nathan D. Champion lying in their bunks.

'Give up, boys,' said one of the invaders, 'we've got you this time,' and fired at Champion, but missed.

Nate Champion, a Texan, grabbed his rifle and drove the pair out under rapid fire. All four fled, but two of the wounded left their coats behind thus giving away their identities. The only one who was arrested was allowed out on bail and left Wyoming.

The next two men to die, Orley Jones and John Tisdale, were men of reputation never accused of rustling, and their murders caused the feeling against the cattle barons to reach frenzied proportions. The unfortunate Tisdale's body was found in his wagon surrounded by blood-stained toys he had been bringing home for his children. Frank Canton, whose horse was found nearby, was arrested – and released.

Now, with the small cattlemen and settlers forming their own organisation, the Northern Wyoming Farmers' and Stock Growers' Association, the cattle barons of the Cheyenne Club plotted over their drinks and cigars the extermination (their exact words) of undesirables in the north of the state. The genocidal list was seventy strong, and to do the job they decided to recruit a gang of gunmen.

In charge was an ex-army officer from Kentucky, now a leading cattleman, Major Frank Wolcott, portly, pompous and something of a strategist, who had been demanding action for some time. The plan was to raise the army for the invasion of Johnson County from outside the state, cut every telegraph line that linked the county to the rest of Wyoming, then head for the county seat of Buffalo. There, the sheriff, 'Red' Angus, his deputies and the local commissioners were to be killed, as all were on the 'wrong' side, after which the 'rustlers' on the death list were to be wiped out one by one.

There was no attempt to keep the plan from the authorities, for among those informed in advance were the Acting Governor, the two US senators and senior officials of the Union Pacific Railroad, who agreed to lay on a special train for the invaders. Horses were bought in Colorado, and recruiting parties headed for Texas, Colorado, Montana and Idaho. Wages, paid by the Wyoming Stock Growers' Association, of $5 a day were offered, plus expenses, and a bonus of $50 for each Regulator for every rustler killed. And each of them was insured for $3000.

So it came about that one April morning in 1892, a Pullman reached the Union Pacific depot at Casper, Wyoming, which disgorged some fifty-two heavily armed and apparently determined men, nearly half of them Texans.

Immediately below Wolcott in rank were Frank Canton and Luther 'Tom' Smith (not to be confused with Tom Smith of Abilene), a badge-toting gunman who had once, it was said, shot seven Negroes in a race riot without lowering his rifle.

Also with the party were two newsmen, Sam Clover of the *Chicago Herald*, and the city editor of the *Cheyenne Sun*, both of whom believed what they had been told. The gunmen travelled in a different part of the train to the Wyoming stockmen, who after all, were 'gentlemen'. This led to trouble when Canton entered the private car and Wolcott ordered him out, and the resulting quarrel on the ride to Casper led to Wolcott's resignation. In the event, Canton's leadership was to prove so ineffectual that the major gradually resumed command.

The invaders headed first for a ranch owned by two of them, confusingly bearing the same name as the man murdered on his way home with Christmas presents, Tisdale. Instead of heading next day for Buffalo as planned, they decided instead to tackle an alleged band of rustlers at the KC ranch fifteen miles away, the band turning out to be Nate Champion and his friend Nick Ray, both on the death list. With them were two trappers who had spent the night with them to shelter from a storm.

The invaders surrounded the cabin, out of which came the trappers one by one, heading respectively for a stream and a barn. They were captured, but freed. Then Ray emerged, to be greeted with a fusillade, and as he crawled back dying towards the hut, Nate Champion appeared, and dragged him back in by the collar with one hand as he loosed off with his six-shooter with the other.

Then began one of the most heroic episodes in the history of the West. All day long Nate Champion kept his attackers at bay, and, even more remarkably, found time to leave his friends an account of the action. It began:

Me and Nick was getting breakfast when the attack took place. Two men was with us – Bill Jones and another man. The old man went after water and did not come back. His friend went to see what was the matter and he did not come back. Nick started out and I told him to look out, that I thought there was someone at the stable and would not let them come back.

Nick is shot but not dead yet. He is awful sick. I must go and wait on him.

It is now about two hours since the first shot. Nick is still alive.

They are still shooting and are all around the house. Boys, there is bullets coming in here like hail.

Them fellows is in such shape I can't get at them. They are shooting from the stable and river and back of the house.

Nick is dead. He died about 9 o'clock.

The day wore on and Nate wrote that he saw smoke down at the stable. 'I think they have fired it. I don't think they intend to let me get away this time.' He confessed to the 'Boys' who would read it that he felt pretty lonesome and wished there was someone with him so that they could watch all sides at once. Finally, the besiegers pushed a wagonload of hay up to the cabin and set it alight. Nate's last entries were before and after this ultimate step:

21
Nate Champion (second from left), the supreme hero of the Johnson County war. Rustler or cowboy, his heroic day-long stand and final death at the hands of some fifty 'invaders' is one of the great epics of the West.

Well, they have just got through shelling the house like hell. I heard them splitting wood. I guess they are going to fire the house tonight. I think I will make a break when night comes, if alive. It's not night yet.

The house is all fire. Goodbye, boys, if I never see you again.

He signed his name, then dashed out of the back door of his burning cabin, firing a shot from his rifle as the first bullet hit him. He fell riddled with twenty-seven more, some of them in his valiant heart.

They found and read his diary, removed a mention of Frank Canton, then pinned a card on his bloody vest, which read 'CATTLE THIEVES, BEWARE'.

Some hours earlier Nate Champion had seen two men ride by, who were pursued by the invaders, but escaped. He could not know, and his killers did not know, that these two had ridden to Buffalo, which was soon up in arms. Sheriff Angus got no help from the National Guard or from nearby Fort McKinney, and found that the wires had been cut when he tried to get a message to the governor. So he raised a posse and headed for the invaders.

They, meanwhile, had enjoyed a hot meal after their exertions, had sent two badly wounded men back to Casper, and were heading towards Buffalo through the night, not as pleased with themselves as they had been. They were even less pleased when a rider warned them of the happenings at Buffalo, and retreated to the TA ranch which they had just left. The town was becoming an armed camp, settlers who were determined when they arrived, becoming even more so when plots to kill Red Angus became known.

22
Major Frank Wolcott, the portly, pompous leader of the Johnson County Invaders.

23
Sheriff William 'Red' Angus, one of those on the death list of the invaders, who managed to turn the tables on them.

At the TA the invaders rapidly entrenched themselves so securely that only lack of food could be guaranteed to defeat them. But by mid-morning they were surrounded by a furious army of settlers and small ranchers, under Angus. This was on 11 April, and on the 12th, the wires were working again long enough for the governor to be alerted. Washington and then the President himself were told that a state of insurrection existed in Johnson County and because only the cattle barons' side of the story reached the White House, the word went out to rescue the invaders from their embarrassing predicament.

Three troops of the 6th US Cavalry headed to the TA ranch with no sympathy for the invaders. Drama and tragedy turned to farce as Major Wolcott and his men, having eaten their last meal, as they thought, were preparing to break out and heard the sound of a trumpet. 'Gentlemen, it is the troops,' said Wolcott, who agreed minutes later to surrender to Colonel Horn, but to 'that man', Red Angus, 'never!'

Away went the prisoners in what amounted to protective custody, and after months of farcical imprisonment and almost as farcical legal proceedings, the case against the invaders was dropped in January 1893. Only the murders of Champion and Ray led to criminal charges, but the key witnesses, the two trappers, had been bribed and sent out of the state, which wrecked the case.

Despite the expense of the invasion, the cattle barons felt smugly certain that they had done the right thing, and Frank Canton dared to write in his autobiography, *Frontier Trails* (1930): 'We made it [Johnson County] safe for an honest man to live in that county and enjoy the fruits of his labour.'

Fortunately for common decency, the homesteaders and their cowboy allies were the winners in the long run, for the cattle barons never regained their grip on the range, and their party, the Republicans, lost the 1892 elections. Those on the stockmen's side who had been rustlers learned discretion,

24

The Johnson County invaders after their defeat. They were never punished for their crimes, but the settlers were the moral victors. Note killer Frank Canton, a gunfighter who switched from crime to 'legal' work.

while in the end ranchers great and small, along with farmers, managed to co-exist and finally even got along well together. As for Nate Champion, among the songs of the Johnson County war the cowboys sang to their herds was one based on his diary (how it managed to survive is truly remarkable). If Texas's part in the war had been a shaming one, at least the one great hero was also a Texan. For the ordinary people of Wyoming, Nate had been their champion indeed.

3 BAD MEN AND WORSE

. . . several drunken men came in and began to curse Texans. I said to the nearest one, 'I'm a Texan.' He began to curse me and threatened to slap me over. To his surprise I pulled my pistol, and he promptly pulled his . . . He fired one shot and ran but I shot at him as he started, the ball hitting him in the mouth, knocking out several teeth and coming out behind his left ear.

The Life of John Wesley Hardin as Written by Himself

The brotherhood of deadly men who excelled in the use of the pistol shared a common bond: they were killers. But the thing that set them apart both among themselves and their contemporaries was their motivation. Some men killed for gain or to survive, and others, notably lawmen, because they had no alternative. But it is the so-called 'bad men' or 'gunmen' of the West who feature in this chapter.

Down the years they have been variously described as ruthless killers, sadistic psychopaths, and by some as misunderstood 'Robin Hoods' compelled to take up crime and risk outlawry to fight oppression and corruption. Perhaps, but somewhere in the middle of those two extremes lie the real 'bad' and 'good-bad' men of the Old West.

The West has itself inspired innumerable bad man legends. One of the most persistent is the 'Bad Man from Bodie', an awesome being who could outshoot, outshout, outfight, outgouge and out-everything anybody else ever did. Whether the residents of Bodie (now a Californian ghost town) appreciated such a reputation is not known, but in its day the town itself was very tough. By the mid 1860s according to some accounts, it housed more than 15,000 miners and was considered so 'wicked' that Mark Twain devoted a whole column to the celebrated 'Bad Man'.

More factually, there was the man who in Western parlance was described as 'a bad man to fool with'. This individual was normally very quiet, kept himself to himself unless provoked, when his reputation as a killer or a tough customer in a fight was fully realised. But what was this man who could, and did, terrorise individuals and whole townships and territories?

At worst he was a Frontier rough, a tough undisciplined character and a menace to others. If he killed people outside the law he was branded a murderer and became a fugitive. That in some cases he killed in self-defence carried little weight with most people if he already had a price on his head. But the real bad man of the West, the outlaw and killer, was basically unscrupulous, a thief and a murderer.

Romantics have worked overtime to stress that indiscriminate killing by Western outlaws was the result of, not the cause of, their outlawry. Some have been immortalised in American folklore, notably the most famous of them all, Jesse James.

Jesse James made his name as a train and bank robber following the end of the American Civil War. Some of his notoriety was shared with his sanctimonious brother Frank, but it is Jesse who has become immortalised as America's Robin Hood. To their friends and partisans the brothers were known affectionately as 'the James Boys' but to the directors of various railroads, victims of hold-ups, relatives of the deceased, and banks that had been 'visited' and 'drawn upon' they were simply 'the James Gang' and large rewards were offered for their capture dead or alive.

The brothers were the sons of Robert James and Zerelda Cole. Alexander Frank (he never used his first name) James was born on 10 January 1843, and Jesse Woodson James on 5 September 1847. Until the outbreak of the Civil War in 1861, both brothers led normal, mundane lives, but the conflict soon changed that. Frank sided with the Confederacy and by 1863 is alleged to have been a member of William Clarke Quantrill's guerrillas.

It is claimed that the James homestead was visited by a number of Kansas militiamen looking for Frank, but he was not found. Angered, the men dragged Jesse's stepfather (their mother had remarried a Dr Samuel) out into the yard and a rope was slung over a branch of a convenient tree. Protesting loudly the good doctor was 'lifted' several times in an effort to get him to talk, but he knew nothing. Evidently Jesse's mother was also mistreated and the young Jesse was whipped for his stubbornness. When the militiamen finally left Jesse swore vengeance and at the first opportunity joined Quantrill.

Little is definitely known of Jesse's wartime activities, but following the end of the war he and others tried to take advantage of the amnesty offered to guerrillas. It is alleged that even as he and some companions rode towards Lexington, Missouri, to surrender they were fired upon by Union soldiers and Jesse was badly wounded. Family members maintain that Jesse's name was not included in the parole because he was thought to be too ill to survive. But he did recover and, according to his son, for sixteen years was a persecuted man. It was because of this reason that he and his brother Frank took up outlawry.

Down the years all manner of crimes have been laid at Jesse and Frank's door, and at this date it would take a great deal of research to unravel fact from fiction. But if we accept even half the stories, the brothers were very active. Because most Missourians had been for the Confederacy during most of the war, they allowed themselves to believe that what the James Gang was doing was almost patriotic, but finally even they realised that 'patriotism' had gone too far.

25

Jesse James; a photograph said to have been taken at Nebraska City in 1875. He had an alarming habit of continually blinking and some claim he suffered from a common frontier complaint, trachoma, or granular conjunctivitis. He was a lethal man when roused.

One such incident occurred on 26 September 1872 when the boys appeared at the annual Kansas City Fair. When they left they took with them the contents of the cashier's safe and got clean away. Later, it was claimed that they were frustrated in their efforts by Wild Bill Hickok. However, Wild Bill's presence at the fair came a day later when a large number of armed and irate Texans (some of whom actually pulled their pistols) were furious when he somewhat provocatively stopped a band from playing *Dixie*!

The robbery at the fair had its humorous aftermath. A local Kansas City reporter wrote a glowing account of the 'heroics' of the brothers who were so impressed that they visited him and offered to present him with

WILLIAM CLARKE QUANTRILL

William Clarke Quantrill, the ill-famed leader of the Confederacy's most infamous band of guerrillas, was born on 31 July 1837, in Canal Dover, Ohio, but by 1857 he was in Kansas. His mother, in a newspaper interview published in 1888, claimed that he was employed as a school teacher, and that he was also a qualified land surveyor. In 1861, following the worst years of the Kansas-Missouri Border wars, Quantrill was torn between his loyalties to the Northern and Southern states. His next move was influenced by an event that took place shortly after the Civil War broke out.

In September 1861, the Confederate General Stirling Price, accompanied by a large force of men, attacked Lexington, Missouri. When he retreated he was pursued by General James Lane, 'the Grim Chieftain of Kansas', a former soldier in the Mexican War (1846-8) and more recently a dedicated fighter against the Missouri Border Ruffians. Believing that Price's march to Lexington had been eased by friendly people along the way, Lane proceeded to treat them as enemies, and his punitive expedition against the Confederate army soon degenerated into a looting spree against civilians. At Osceola, Missouri, he court-martialed and shot nine people and burnt most of the town's buildings. It was this act that prompted Quantrill to throw in his lot with the Confederacy, and ultimately led to a ruthless act of 'reprisal' on his part that was the most memorable of the whole war.

He soon gathered around him a gang of cut-throats and murderers, whose membership included, apart from Frank James and the Youngers, such men as the infamous Bloody Bill Anderson, who became Quantrill's chief lieutenant. By early 1863, Quantrill's name was on everyone's lips and he was hated and feared by those opposed to the rebel cause. It was then that news came that he was again in Kansas. The authorities had been warned that he might attack Lawrence knowing that Lane was there, but the threat was not taken seriously. At the head of more than 400 men Quantrill attacked Lawrence at daybreak on 21 August, looted and burned the town, killing more than 150 men. Lane barely made his escape, and by the time he organised a small force in pursuit, Quantrill was long gone.

By 1864 some of Quantrill's followers were becoming disillusioned by the way the war was going. The excitement they once felt following the 'Black Flag of Quantrill' had gone, and some of them left him. (The Leavenworth *Daily Conservative*, 28 August 1862, described a captured Quantrill flag as a 'cross between a nose bleed and a diaper with a small star sewn on it'. The paper suggested the followers of such a flag should be spanked.) Those that remained loyal accompanied him to Texas where he raided wagon trains, robbed settlements and murdered innocent people. By now even the Confederacy (in whose army he was considered to be a colonel) began to disown him, so he returned to Missouri and then on to Kentucky. When Lee surrendered his Army of Northern Virginia to Grant on 9 April 1865, and the remainder of the Confederacy followed suit, Quantrill realised that time was against him, and decided to surrender.

But Fate as well as time was against him. His command was intercepted and attacked by a contingent of Kentucky Federal guerrillas led by Captain Edward Terrill on 10 May 1865. The Union force cut Quantrill's men to ribbons and he himself was badly wounded. He was taken to the Sisters of Charity Hospital at Louisville where he died on 6 June. The Black Flag would fly no more.

26
William Clarke Quantrill looks mild enough but was the most hated and feared of all the South's guerrilla leaders.

26

27

27
'Bloody Bill' Anderson, Quantrill's faithful lieutenant, who normally rode into action with as many as eight revolvers in his belt, a not uncommon habit among guerrillas on both sides as there was little time in battle to reload. One story about Anderson is that he once tried to hang a man, only to be told that the Queen would see to it that he, too, would hang. 'What Queen?' asked the startled killer. 'Why Queen Victoria, of course,' replied the intended victim. 'She always protects her loyal subjects.' Anderson, reputedly impressed and amused, let the man go.

28

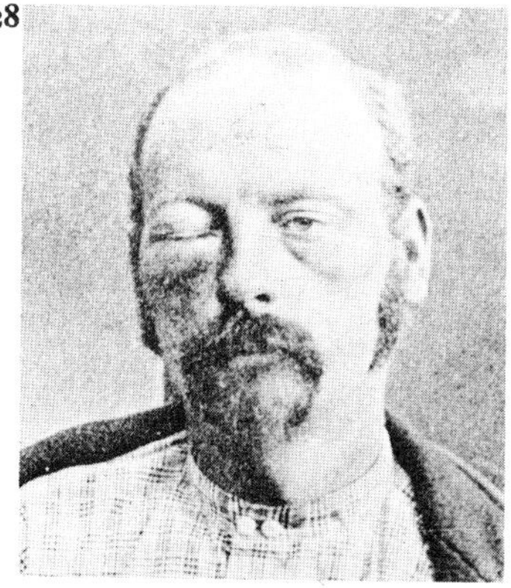

29

28 and 29
Cole and Bob Younger after their capture following the disastrous raid on the Northfield Bank in September 1863.

30

30
The First National Bank at Northfield.

a gold watch. The outcome was noted by the *Ellsworth Reporter* (copying it from a Kansas City paper). The surprised, and considerably frightened journalist thanked them for their offer but refused the watch thinking it was stolen. 'Heck no,' retorted Jesse, 'this'n we bought with our own money!' Still the reporter refused. Pained and puzzled, Jesse looked him straight in the eye and said: 'Well, then perhaps you can name some man around here you want killed?'

By 1876 the notoriety of the James Gang was such that every move they made was widely reported. When they attempted to rob the First National Bank at Northfield, Minnesota, on 7 September, armed and determined citizens shot down a number of the gang (a combination of the Youngers and the Jameses) and Jesse and Frank barely escaped with their lives. Reports of this raid even reached London, where *The Times* in its first story attributed the robbery to one 'James Brothers' but corrected it at a later date.

The Youngers were not so lucky. Cole Younger had ridden with Frank James as a member of Quantrill's guerrillas. In fact both families were near neighbours and the boys had grown up together, and following the Civil War the combined James-Younger gang had been responsible for innumerable robberies. During the disastrous Northfield raid all three of the Younger brothers, Cole, Jim and Bob, were seriously wounded. Two weeks later the three brothers were captured. Bob died in prison in 1889, while Jim and Cole after serving twenty-five years were released in 1901. But within a year James was dead, a suicide, and Cole then joined up with Frank James on a lecture tour decrying the evils of cıime!

By 1882 Jesse James realised only too well that his days as an outlaw were numbered. Although he had changed his name to Thomas Howard, he knew it was only a matter of time before the law or someone anxious for the $25,000 reward caught up with him. His last known letter is dated 22 March and is to a man advertising land for sale. Jesse was anxious to take up farming, but he never got the chance.

On the morning of 3 April at St Joseph, Missouri, he was shot in the back as he stood on a chair adjusting a picture. His cousin Robert Ford, was the murderer, destined to be branded as 'the dirty little coward that shot Mr Howard'.

31
Robert 'Bob' Ford, the cousin of Jesse James, who, on 3 April 1882 became the 'dirty little coward that shot Mr Howard (James's alias) and laid poor Jesse in his grave'.

Once the news got around that Jesse was dead hundreds of people converged on the house and the owner did a roaring trade selling pieces of the floor boards stained with Jesse's blood – although certain uncharitable people alleged that the landlord had unscrupulously dipped the pieces of another board into the blood of an ox in order to meet the demand!

Bob Ford, who was pardoned for his activities with the gang (it was part of a deal he had made with the state governor if Jesse was killed) did not enjoy his new-found fame. Ten years later he was murdered by a man named Ed Kelly whom he had accused of stealing. Ironically, the man who killed Bob Ford was related by marriage to the Youngers.

The James family suffered down the years for the sins of their father. As late as 1899, the Abilene *Chronicle*, in reporting that Jesse James Jr was to play baseball in the city, also noted that he had recently been acquitted on a charge of train robbery. Some claimed that there was reason for suspicion, while others thought his name was sufficient to implicate him in any crime.

Jesse James the man was dead, but controversy raged and still does over Jesse James the legend. Legend still depicts him as a Robin Hood, but to most hard-headed historians he was a villain, basically unstable, violent and a paranoic whose only means of achievement was to resort to robbery and violence. Somewhere in between both views lies the real Jesse James.

* * *

The real Billy the Kid is gradually emerging from lurid legend thanks to the work of modern historians, most notably Robert N. Mullin, whose *The Boyhood of Billy the Kid* has finally proved beyond reasonable doubt that the outlaw's early years were notably uneventful. The latent violence may have been there all the time, but it was circumstance that made it erupt. His short career made marvellous newspaper copy while he was living, and soon after he died hugely popular novels were rushed into print including, it may reasonably be said, *The Authentic Life of Billy the Kid* (1882) by his killer, Pat Garrett. Admittedly, a journalist named Ashman Upson ghosted it, but Garrett made no objections to the flights from fact.

Naturally, readers believed that Billy, aged twelve, had despatched 'a filthy loafer' who had made an insulting remark about his mother, using a pocket knife, 'its blade dripping with gore' after the deed. Naturally, the Upson/Garrett account of how Billy once routed a band of Indians, his pistol belching forth 'a stream of death-laden fire', was treated as gospel. Everything conspired to make the legend of the boy killer accepted fact.

Even Mullin has not solved the problem of Billy's birth and actual surname. He was probably born in New York or Indiana in 1859, his name was Henry, his surname either McCarty or Bonney. He and his older brother Joe and his mother lived for a time in Wichita, Kansas, then moved to Silver City, New Mexico, where young Henry took the surname Antrim, his

32
This portrait of Billy the Kid is the only one all the experts accept as authentic. Made from an old tintype, it is always reproduced as made – in reverse, which explains why Billy is always called a 'left-handed gun' (the title of a Paul Newman movie about the Kid). In fact, he was right-handed.

mother having married a miner of that name. She was a 'jolly Irish lady' according to a neighbour, while her son was no trouble at school and took part in amateur theatricals.

Henry McCarty, as he was known in Silver City, had a brush with the law in September 1875. Legend turned it into a robbery of $70, but it was less dramatic. One 'Sombrero Jack' had stolen some clothes from two Chinamen as a joke and gave Henry and another boy the bundle to hide. Probably to teach young McCarty a lesson, the sheriff locked him in jail. Henry, who refused to name the other boy,

THE DALTONS

Rivalling the James Boys as bank robbers with 'gang' status were the Daltons, long-time favourites with novelists and film scriptwriters. The four Dalton brothers who achieved a dubious immortality were Grat, Emmett, Bob and Bill, and they were among fifteen children born to Lewis and Adeline Dalton.

It was claimed that their mother, Adeline Younger Dalton, was related to the Youngers, but she did not like to talk about it, and for many years the family remained respectable despite sneering comments about their kinship with the Youngers.

One of their sons, Frank, served for a period as a deputy US marshal acting under the orders of the formidable Judge Isaac C. Parker. He was shot and killed in 1887 while trying to arrest three whiskey peddlers west of Fort Smith. Grat was hired to replace his brother, and later Bob was also employed as a deputy marshal. Bill, meantime, had married and settled down, while Emmett was working on a ranch.

The four brothers became outlaws for various reasons. Emmett got a little too interested in the art of horse-stealing; Bob killed a man named Charlie Montgomery over a woman; Grat was suspected of selling stolen livestock; and Bob lost his badge when it was found that he had been involved with him. Later, Bill was implicated with his brothers and was believed to have planned most of their robberies.

Following a couple of years with various organisations the four brothers joined together and planned what they hoped would be their biggest raid on their home town Coffeyville.

They rode into the place on 5 October 1892, heavily disguised in the hope that no one would recognise them. But things did not quite work according to plan – the plan was to rob two banks at the same time.

While Bob and Emmett were helping themselves to cash at the First National Bank, they were recognised by a passer-by who rushed into the town square shouting: 'The Daltons! The Daltons!' and soon the place was teeming with people who had armed themselves with their own weapons or those made available by the local store.

Meantime, at the Condon Bank, Grat, accompanied by Tim Evans and Dick Broadwell, was delayed because the bank vault had a time lock. This delay gave the citizens time to station themselves and moments later they started shooting. The Daltons joined in.

Within moments the town square was one blue haze of powder smoke, and when it cleared and the noise of the shooting had died away, four citizens had been killed, and all the Daltons with the exception of Emmett were dead. He survived and was sentenced to life imprisonment at the Lansing, Kansas, penitentiary, but fourteen years later he was pardoned and spent his remaining years in California, where he became an 'adviser' on Western pictures and the author of several books and articles on law and order! He died in Los Angeles in 1937.

33
Bob and Grat Dalton, dead or dying, being held up by officers in Coffeyville following their botched raid of 5 October 1892. It was reported in the press that: 'One of our banking institutions was visited yesterday by the firm of Dalton Brothers for the purpose of closing large accounts. When the transaction was completed they had been paid in full with interest compounded.'

34
Three dead Daltons and Dick Broadwell (right) stretched out and handcuffed even in death following a hectic session in the 'powder and ball' stakes.

became very nervous about his imagined fate and escaped via a chimney for Arizona, where, contrary to the legends, he worked unsensationally as a ranch hand and was dubbed the Kid, or Kid Antrim. Then, on 17 August 1877, he killed his first man.

Burly Frank 'Windy' Cahill enjoyed bullying the Kid and that day he called him (oddly) a pimp and a son-of-a-bitch. The pair wrestled and the slight Kid was thrown. He drew his gun, an eye-witness later stating: 'He had no choice, he had to use his "equaliser".' Cahill died the next day. Choice or no, the Kid was arrested. He escaped, but it is not certain how.

The next key event was his signing on as William Bonney with Englishman John Tunstall some time in the fall of 1877. The events that followed, the murder of Tunstall and the Lincoln County war, have been related in Chapter 2, where Billy was left after coming to the fore in the final stages of the five day pitched battle in Lincoln itself.

After the battle, and with Tunstall's partner, the unfortunate McSween, dead, the war was virtually over. Great wrong had triumphed over lesser wrong. Many of the rougher Dolan supporters now indulged in an orgy of killing, robbery, looting and rape, while Billy and friends took to rustling but not raping. Then into New Mexico came a new governor, General Lew (*Ben Hur*) Wallace, his famous book almost completed, and his mission the unenviable one of restoring order. Billy, with a string of murder warrants against him, wanted to give himself up and testify against other 'war' veterans, and Wallace received a letter from him stating that W. H. Bonney wished to meet him.

The pair met dramatically in secret and Billy got his promise of a pardon. Soon he was in technical custody and he helped indict John Dolan, the arch enemy of Tunstall and McSween, for murder though, as we have seen, Dolan had too many friends in high places to be touched. Meanwhile, the district attorney objected to a pardon for the Kid, who therefore decided to leave his loose confinement and return to crime at the head of his gang. He especially enjoyed stealing from John Chisum's herds after the great cattle king refused, even under the threat of Billy's gun, to pay up for services rendered in the Lincoln County war.

By mid 1880, the gang was becoming a menace, and the new sheriff of Lincoln County, Pat Garrett, a friend of Billy's, went into action against him even before starting his official term of office. The six foot four inch sheriff's traps failed until, on 19 December, Tom O'Folliard, leading the band to Fort Sumner, was killed. Then, on the 23rd, Garrett and his posse cornered the five survivors at a house at Stinking Springs and Charlie Bowdre was killed. The rest gave in.

Billy was tried for Sheriff Brady's murder in April 1881, found guilty and sentenced to hang on 13 May. He was imprisoned in the old Dolan and Murphy store, by now the County Jail. On 28 April, while Garrett was away, either – as he later claimed – tax collecting, or, more interestingly, getting carpenters to build a scaffold, Billy pulled off his greatest coup. One of his guards, Robert Olinger, was across the road in charge of the other prisoners as they ate a meal in a restaurant, and Billy asked the other, J. W.

35
The Lincoln County Courthouse as it appeared after its restoration in 1939. It was from this building that Billy the Kid made his sensational escape when under sentence of death.

Bell, to escort him to the privy in the yard. On the way back, Billy slipped his handcuffs from his small hands, an old trick of his, and, swinging his shackles at Bell, knocked him down, then shot him with his own gun or, as many believe, with one hidden in the privy by a friend, Sam Corbet. Corbet had been allowed to visit Billy daily and is said to have slipped him a note on which was a single word – privy.

After killing Bell, the Kid grabbed a shotgun from Garrett's office and waited at a window for Olinger. 'Hello, Bob!' Billy shouted as the doomed deputy came running to find out the meaning of the shot. He looked up at the balcony and Billy fired, then laughed, smashed the shotgun and hurled it down beside his second victim.

The elated Kid later rode off, still shackled on one leg, having shaken hands all round first, apologised to the corpse of Bell, so a witness later related, and touched Olinger's body with the tip of his boot. 'You are not going to round me up again,' he informed the body.

Even the anti-Tunstall/McSween Santa Fe *New Mexican* expressed grudging admiration for Billy's astonishing escape, but his days were now numbered. In less than three months he would be dead.

Garrett, humiliated by events, was hampered by the fact that most citizens, American and Mexican, were on Billy's side. But on 14 July 1881, he rode to Fort Sumner to check out a rumour that the Kid was in the vicinity. He had two deputies with him.

On reaching Fort Sumner,

36
Pat Garrett, Sheriff of Lincoln County, who finally killed his erstwhile friend, Billy the Kid.

Garrett called at the cabin of Pete Maxwell, a rancher whom he knew and who was likely to know the whereabouts of the Kid. Leaving his men outside, he went into Maxwell's bedroom. It was past midnight.

Billy had been at a dance and, feeling hungry, took a knife and headed for Maxwell's home, where he had been told there was a quarter of butchered steer hanging on the porch. He was shoeless and hatless.

He spotted the two strangers, drew his gun and slipped into Maxwell's bedroom to ask him who they were. He did not spot Pat Garrett, sitting on the edge of Maxwell's bed.

As Billy asked: 'Who are they, Pete?' Maxwell whispered to Garrett: 'That's him!' The Kid began to retreat, crying: '*Quién es? Quién es?*' [Who's that? Who's that?]. Garrett drew his pistol and shot him dead.

His friends gave him a fine funeral. There was an old Spanish custom that people took it in turns the night before the ceremony to stay with the body and pray, and his many friends around Fort Sumner saw to it that the custom was followed. Then they buried him in the old government cemetery at the fort.

The killing did not make Pat Garrett widely popular and he was even accused of shooting an unarmed man, which was a ridiculous charge, as Billy would hardly have risked going anywhere without his gun in his final years. But naturally, as the killer of the nationally famous Kid, he was a made man, holding down good jobs, including one as a customs collector, a post given him by an admiring President Theodore Roosevelt, who met him at a luncheon. His career took a turn for the worse when a ranch in New Mexico started to fail and he began to drink heavily. In 1908, he was killed by one Wayne Brazil, after feuding with him, the killer being acquitted.

By then Billy the Kid had become one of the West's great legends and the myth of his twenty-one killings for each of his twenty-one years was firmly established. Environment, events and his character made him a highly dangerous outlaw, but there was nothing of the homicidal maniac about him. He was no Robin Hood and it is understandable that serious historians have refused to allow the slightest suggestion that he was, but neither was he remotely a monster. As Jeff Burton has written: 'Better men have been hanged, worse men by far have gone on to be elected to high political office.'

As for his death tally, up to the time of McSween's death he had 'helped' in at least five factional killings, but Cahill was the only man he had killed while acting alone. His grand total may have been less than ten.

And then there was Texas.

37
William P. Longley, photographed just before his execution. Before he dropped through the trap, he said: 'I see a good many enemies around, and mighty few friends.'

Two of Texas's most famous bad men were William P. Longley and John Wesley Hardin. In many respects their early lives and misdeeds are similar, for both of them blamed the Civil War for their problems.

William P. Longley was born in 1851, and was almost ten years of age when the Civil War started. At fifteen he was said to be already six feet in height and a popular pupil at the local school house. Like most boys of his generation it was claimed that 'he could ride before he could walk' and he had studied 'triggernometry'. And it was this latter accomplishment that soon got him into trouble.

Following the assassination of Abraham Lincoln on 14 April 1865 and the implementation of the dreaded Northern Government's 'Reconstruction' policy, Texas like most other Southern states, was invaded by an army of licensed scavengers anxious to ensure both that the new policy would work and that they would profit by it. To protect these 'carpetbaggers' as the South scathingly called them, the Union Army reinforced its troops with various state police forces, manned mostly by Negroes under the command of white officers.

Few of the older Negroes became involved with the state police, but the younger ones eagerly joined, for it seemed to some of them a good chance to get back at their former masters. The result was predictable.

Bill Longley and the state police soon fell out and, following an insult against his father, he swiftly killed one of the Negro police and was soon a wanted man. Texas legend has it that Longley's very name terrified the Negroes.

For more than ten years Bill Longley's name was on the lips of most Texans and finally, when he was captured and put on trial for his life in 1877 for the murder of a man named Wilson Anderson, he was credited by the press with having killed thirty-two men, most of them blacks.

Sentenced to hang, Longley had to wait more than a year before the legal wranglings were ironed out, during which time he bombarded the state governor with letters. In particular he was very angry that his rival for fame as the premier gunman of Texas, John Wesley Hardin, for whom he had nothing but contempt, had been arrested and sentenced to a long jail term whereas he was to die. On 11 October 1878, he was hanged at Giddings, Texas. Even then there were those who doubted that he was dead. The drop was long (twelve feet) and the rope slipped so that his feet touched the ground. Swiftly he was lifted up in the arms of spectators, the rope adjusted, and he was allowed to drop again. Eleven minutes later he was pronounced dead. But there were many who believed that he had been spirited away to live out his life in obscurity. As late as 1915 when the *Lusitania* was torpedoed, someone claimed that among the passengers was a South American cattlebuyer named William P. Longley!

Although Longley had no liking for John Wesley Hardin (and they are believed to have met only once) there was a similarity in their backgrounds and in their early exploits. Born in 1853, Hardin was always in trouble. He was barely eight years old when the Civil War started, and when it ended his home state of Texas was in the grip of the Northern Forces

38
John Wesley Hardin, named after the great Methodist, but destined to be one of the West's most notorious killers. From a photograph made about 1876-7.

of Occupation. Like Longley he objected to the ex-slaves' reaction towards the whites and the man who was later said (but never proved) to have 'forty notches' to his credit was soon wanted for murder.

By 1871 he already had a reputation and this was furthered when he joined a herd owned by Columbus Carrol on its way to Abilene, Kansas, then the centre of the Texas cattle trade Hardin had killed his first man in 1868 and by the spring of 1871 the total had risen to twelve. During his brief period in Kansas, he is believed to have killed another eight men. He shot it out with some Mexican herders on his way into town, and when his friend, William Cohron, was murdered, Hardin and Cohron's brother set out to avenge him. Together they tracked the killer, one Juan Bideno, to Sumner City, Kansas, and shot him dead in the dining-room of the Southwestern Hotel.

Soon afterwards Hardin killed a man in Abilene as he sat on his bed reading a newspaper. He fired through the wall killing him instantly, commenting later that the man's 'snoring' disturbed him. None the less, this notorious bad man hastily fled from town one jump ahead of the marshal, Will Bill Hickok, with whom until then he had been quite friendly.

Back in Texas and still on the run, Hardin celebrated his twenty-first birthday on 26 May 1874 by shooting and killing a deputy sheriff named Charles Webb in Comanche. The details are obscure, but Hardin's account suggests that the two men had just met when Webb shot him in the side. Hardin immediately pulled his pistol (a Smith and Wesson 'American') and shot Webb through the left cheek. At that moment some of Hardin's friends commenced shooting at the deputy. Hardin surrendered to sheriff John Karnes, but when a lynch mob materialised he made his escape.

Three years later, following constant pursuit by the Rangers, he was captured at Pensacola, Florida. Even as the lawmen moved in Hardin tried to pull a gun on them, but it jammed in his braces and he was arrested without a shot being fired.

Hardin remained in jail until 17 February 1894, when he was discharged and granted a full pardon and restoration to citizenship. His wife Jane died before his release and possibly because of this he lost all will to succeed at anything. Certainly, his activities when he left jail suggest that he did not care

39
Clay Allison in one of his more sober moments.

too much about himself or others. A smattering of law he had learned in jail enabled him to hang out his lawyer's shingle in Gonzales, Texas, but he soon moved farther west. In El Paso he finally met his destiny when a local policeman named John Selman came up behind him in the Acme saloon and blew his brains out. The once notorious gunman never got a chance to draw his gun.

One man who remains an enigma is Clay Allison, who, some claimed, once rode his horse down the streets of a cowtown stark naked except for a pair of six-shooters, in an attempt to emulate Lady Godiva. Describing himself on one occasion as a 'shootist', which in that context meant gunman or gunfighter, he made it known to many that he was indeed a 'bad man to fool with'.

Born in 1840 near Waynesboro, Wayne County, Tennessee, Robert A. Clay Allison spent his first twenty-one years as a labourer on his parents' farm. When the Civil War broke out Tennessee was divided in its loyalties between North and South, and Clay chose to become a Confederate.

He was found to be mentally unstable and, after serving a year in the Tennessee Light Artillery, he was discharged. The report alleged that perhaps because of a blow on the skull years before he was now prone to part epileptic and part maniacal behaviour with suicidal tendencies. It is claimed that he shot a soldier in the Third Illinois Cavalry for breaking one of his mother's favourite serving jugs during a raid on the homestead at the time Clay was recovering from his dismissal from the army. What is not explained is how he managed to save his own neck from the soldier's companions.

The remainder of his war was spent with a Tennessee cavalry regiment during which time he is also alleged to have been an occasional scout or spy. Following the war he drifted to Texas where he became a cowboy, riding for the embryo cattle kings, Oliver Loving and his partner Charles Goodnight. As time went by Allison's reputation as a fighting man and a gunman began to grow. Few of the men who came up against him were his equal except for one, Mace Bowman, who by all accounts beat him to the draw so many times he tired of the sport and decided to use live ammunition. Legend asserts that they then started shooting at each other's feet to make the other dance faster, but miraculously neither was hurt! Allison was violent and unpredictable with scant regard for law and order. Several attempts were made to arrest him, but he seems to have avoided it. A number of killings, including those of several Negroes were also laid at his door but not proved.

It is a part of Western legend that Clay Allison once invaded Dodge City, Kansas, and tackled its policemen, all of whom were afraid of him. One version had it that Wyatt Earp arrested him, another that Bat Masterson avoided him (rather than have innocent people hurt) and still another that Bat's younger brother Jim actually arrested Clay because he was drunk. Another, and possibly the truth, states that Allison did meet both Earp and Masterson and that the meeting was friendly.

With age, however, Allison seems to have calmed down a little. In 1878 he married. He had two daughters, one of whom was born shortly after his death.

The end came for Clay on 1 July 1887. He had borrowed a wagon and loaded it up with supplies for his ranch and about forty miles from Pecos one of the sacks of grain fell off. He stopped to retrieve it. Somehow he fell beneath the wagon and the horses moved off, and one of the rear wheels passed over his neck. He died soon afterwards in great agony, an ignominious end for a man who having lived by the gun for so long no doubt expected to die by it.

Among the bad men who achieved fame ostensibly as 'good men' was the notorious conman extraordinary, Henry Plummer. His origin is uncertain, for some claim he came from England and others that he was born in Boston. However, in 1852 he was in California where he joined the gold-seekers. Within a year he had joined one Henry Hyer and opened the 'Empire Bakery' in Nevada City, California, where he soon became a much respected citizen.

Such was Plummer's personality that he found no difficulty in convincing people of his sincerity, and his gentlemanly manners and courtesies to women quickly found an eager response. By 1857, when he was marshal of Nevada City, he was also being considered as prospective Democratic candidate for the forthcoming assembly, but at the last moment his supporters chose another man, which did not please Plummer one bit.

Then came the first of the events that were eventually to lead to a vigilante necktie party. A German named Vedder had an attractive wife whose charms proved irresistible to Henry Plummer and soon he was having an affair with her. One day the German came home unexpectedly and found the pair of them in bed. Evidently the man was unarmed, but Plummer shot him dead just the same. Sentenced to ten years in jail, Plummer, with the help of friends, successfully petitioned the state governor and was released on the grounds that he was 'consumptive'.

After a short period, when he was again in the bakery business, he got into further trouble with the law and on one occasion he tried to rob a stagecoach. But the barrel of his pistol – which was not secured properly by its retaining wedge – fell off, at which point the driver whipped up his horses and escaped.

When Plummer finally quit

California he managed to avoid pursuit by informing a gullible editor that he and a companion had been hanged in Washington Territory by vigilantes for the murder of two men. By 1863, following several other scrapes and the killing of a saloon owner, he arrived in Bannack accompanied by his wife and a man named Jack Cleveland.

Bannack had started life as the 'Grasshopper Diggings' when gold was discovered at Grasshopper Creek, a tributary of Beaverhead River in Washington Territory. Once the discovery was verified thousands swarmed into the area – later to become Idaho Territory and part of present-day Montana. As with other boom towns, outlawry and thievery ran hand in hand and the crack of the revolver was a common sound. During this period of unrest Henry Plummer managed to ingratiate himself with the more law-abiding citizens, none of whom had any idea that the upright, smiling man of integrity was anything but respectable, and during the first election of county officers, on 24 May 1863, Plummer was elected sheriff.

At the time of this coup, Plummer had a 100-strong gang of road agents (highwaymen), who relieved local miners and other travellers of their possessions. He ran lodging houses near the mines, staffed with his men, and any stagecoach worth robbing was marked. The gang wore ties in a special knot to identify fellow members and called themselves the 'Innocents'. So it was that Plummer, drunk with power, became a veritable Napoleon of crime. But, finally, suspicions were aroused, vigilantes were raised and an 'innocent' confessed.

The citizens took action. Plummer was dressing when he opened the door to urgent knocking, and even had he been able to pull his pistol it would have proved useless. He was swiftly overpowered as were two of his companions who were arrested in other parts of the town.

Plummer's companions, Ned Ray and Buck Stinson, begged for their lives and both died badly cursing their captors. But Plummer remained calm. Just before the fatal noose was adjusted over the beam of the gallows, he asked that they give him a good drop. The men, many of them former friends, some of whom even then doubted his guilt but were overruled by the majority, agreed and hoisted him high above their shoulders. The rope was drawn tight and at a word they suddenly dropped him. The rope snapped tight and he died very quickly without much struggle.

In contrast to Plummer, another man whom the vigilantes of Montana hanged less than a year later, Joseph Alfred 'Jack' Slade, was not a bad man in the sense that Plummer was. Rather he was more the 'good bad man' so beloved by romantics, for in his sober periods he was the perfect gentleman, conscientious and reliable when given a task to do. But when drunk, which in his later years became an all too frequent occurrence, he was a veritable terror. It was said of Slade that far from being the instrument of the Devil he was the servant of the Almighty (some people feared him more!) for his presence in town drunk on any

40
Joseph Alfred 'Jack' Slade, whose exploits as a superintendent on the Overland Stage Lines made him more feared than 'the Almighty'. From a sketch by an unknown artist.

Sunday guaranteed a full congregation at the local church when the dreaded cry: 'Slade's drunk!' filled every pew, as each man 'hunted a hole to hide in'!

Perhaps because of his conflicting and at times unpredictable character, Slade was able to command men as he did. He was born in Illinois in 1824 and served in the Mexican War (1846-8) before moving West where he is believed to have spent some time in Kansas. In the late 1850s Jack was hired as a line superintendent for the Central Overland California and Pike's Peak Express Company.

Slade's responsibility was the route known as the Sweetwater Division, which began at the Upper California Crossing of the South Plate River and extended as far as Rocky Ridge. During his period as superintendent he heard that one Jules Bene (sometimes called Reni) was collaborating with outlaws and disposing of company stock.

Bene, a French Canadian was the founder of Julesburg, at that time a small trading post on the South Plate River not far from Denver, Colorado.

When Benjamin Ficklin, the general superintendent for the company, heard of Bene's alleged activities he ordered Slade to investigate. Trouble between Slade and Bene was not long in coming. Bene refused to submit to Slade's authority and even tried to kill him by firing several loads of buckshot into him. But miraculously Slade survived and only the timely arrival of Ficklin saved him from being hanged by Slade's outraged friends. As it was he escaped with his life by agreeing to leave the country. Slade recovered but nursed a grudge against Bene, and the latter made the fatal mistake of coming back . . .

When Slade caught up with him, the unfortunate Bene was tied to a fence post and shot full of holes before Slade put the barrel of his pistol in his mouth and blew his brains out. After which, it is alleged, Slade cut off his ears and pickled them, using one of them as a watch fob.

Slade's reputation by now was such that when Mark Twain met him during an epic stagecoach ride west in 1861 (which he later recounted in *Roughing It*), he was rather surprised to find that he did not possess two heads. As it was he warmed to him 'despite his awful history'. Of Slade's legendary marksmanship, Twain noted humorously:

Slade was a matchless marksman with a navy revolver. The legends say that one morning at Rocky Ridge, when he was feeling comfortable, he saw a man approaching who had offended him some days before – observe the fine memory he had for matters like that – and, 'Gentlemen,' said Slade, drawing, 'it is a good twenty-yard shot – I'll clip the third button on his coat!' Which he did. The bystanders all admired it. And they all attended the funeral too.

But all was not well with Slade. He lost his job with the stage line after shooting up Fort Halleck, and moved to Montana with his wife. Here he made an attempt at ranching, but his drinking grew worse, and finally, following several rampages in Virginia City, he was hanged by the vigilantes on 10 March 1864.

Not all the so-called bad men set out to ride the owlhoot trail.

41
Slade's Virginia Dale Stage Station and Ranch was named for his remarkable wife. Soon after they hanged Slade, she arrived and her rage frightened many of his executioners. She removed his body, but not before she accused his friends of allowing him to be hanged like a dog when they should have shot him like a man. Slade's body was placed in a tin coffin, filled with alcohol to preserve it, and his wife set off for his home town of Carlyle, Illinois, for the burial. But by the time she reached Salt Lake City, Utah, she had changed her mind and had him buried there in a Mormon cemetery on 20 July 1864.

42
Sam Bass was not the world's most successful outlaw. The photograph shows him in Indiana aged sixteen. A passionate lover of horse-racing, he found being a cowboy dull and took to crime, pulling off one major train robbery before the Texas Rangers caught up with him. He died in 1878 on his twenty-seventh birthday. He actually does seem to have been that rarity, a robber who sometimes gave to the poor.

43
Black Jack Ketchum's fame as an outlaw was overshadowed by the notoriety he achieved in death. Sentenced to be hanged, when his body dropped through the trap, the weights and the drop had not been calculated properly and his head was torn from his body.

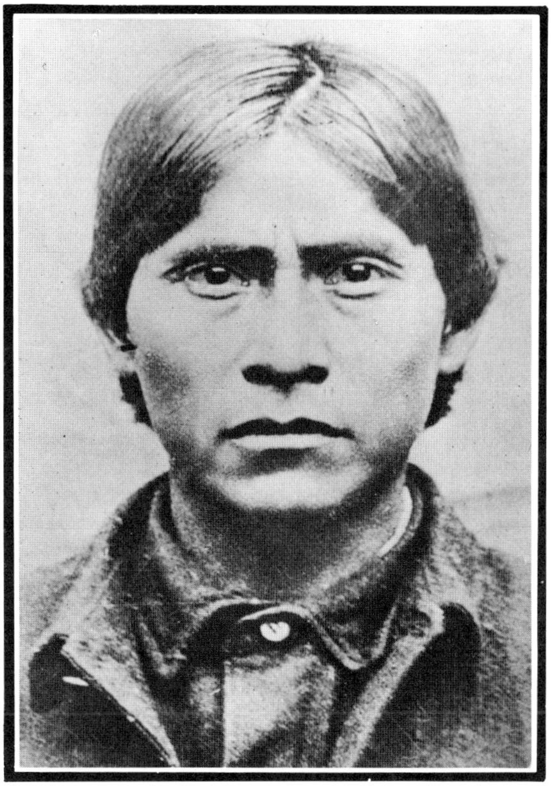

44
The Apache Kid was a loyal scout for the US Army until his treatment at the hands of whites turned him into a ruthless outlaw. Many claimed to have killed him, but after waging a successful one man war against the United States, he vanished into the wilds of Mexico.

For some it was largely due to circumstances beyond their control. Some say that such a man was Tom Horn, erstwhile army scout and peace officer, who ended up a convicted murderer and alleged assassin. His early life is obscure, but by the late 1870s he had acquired a knowledge of the cattle business and was able to speak Spanish. He is also credited with being able to understand the Chiracahua Apache dialect and for this reason was soon employed as a scout, working at times for Generals George Crook and later Nelson A. Miles.

In the late 1880s he got involved in the mining business but this did not last long. According to his own statements he was employed as a Pinkerton detective between 1890 and 1894, following which he may well have become a range detective, a job which with his experience of tracking must have been very simple. Horn served in the Spanish-American War in 1898, but was not in any of the fighting due to a severe attack of fever which necessitated his return home.

Finally, just at the turn of the century, he was back once more in Wyoming where he again sought employment as a detective. Wyoming at this time, less than eight years after the Johnson County war of 1892, was still suffering from disputes between the little cattlemen and the larger concerns. As a 'stock detective' (which some derogatorily called 'thief killer') Horn was responsible for keeping an eye on anything suspicious and reporting it at once to his employers. However, if anyone decided to shoot it out, then Tom Horn was the man to oblige them.

Unfortunately for him, his awesome reputation, alleged by some to have been self-inspired, proved a great handicap. Several killings were laid at his door but never proved. However, one day in July 1901 something happened that was to have serious consequences for Tom Horn.

The trouble began in the February of that year when two homesteaders, Jim Miller and Kels Nickell, fell out. In the quarrel Miller stabbed Nickell but did not kill him. Already in dispute, both families now actively hated each other. Tom Horn was known to both of them but seemed aloof from their fight. Then in July the body of fourteen - year - old Willie Nickell was found near a gate three-quarters of a mile from his home.

At the inquest several days later it was hinted that the killing was the work of the Millers but no evidence was offered. Even Tom Horn was suspect but no motive was discovered. Just when it seemed that the boy's murder would end up as yet another of the unsolved killings, then common, a lady friend of Horn's asserted that the boy had been killed by the Millers; but her evidence was not accepted as conclusive. It was then that Joe Lafors, a shadowy and sinister character, and himself a noted stock detective (but at that time a deputy US marshal) based at Cheyenne, next appeared on the scene and set about the task of breaking the Nickell case.

Lafors and Horn knew each other but not intimately, so when Lafors offered Horn a job working with a cattle ranch in Montana he eagerly accepted. He broke his journey at Omaha and promptly got drunk (a habit which had often landed him in trouble). When sober, Horn was very quiet and inoffensive, but drunk he became boastful and made outrageous claims. He was so drunk that he lost his outfit and had to return to his base for another, and while there received a note from Lafors asking him to meet him in Cheyenne, where, Joe said, his new employer would be also.

Horn stopped off at Laramie on the way, again got drunk and by the time he reached Cheyenne he was almost paralytic. Lafors was delighted. He had worked hard both to get Horn in Cheyenne and also drunk, and had merely used the Montana job as an excuse. During the next few hours Lafors kept Horn well supplied with liquor and plied him with questions about his activities and asked for his opinion of the Nickell case. When Lafors finally asked him how he killed the boy, Horn went into great detail and on the basis of his 'drunken confession' he was arrested and tried for murder.

45
Tom Horn divides opinion in Wyoming to this day. Here he awaits his execution in jail. Some claim that he is holding the rope that later hanged him – for a murder he may not have committed.

All through the trial Horn protested his innocence and others, too, pleaded for him, but in vain. Lafors' evidence was accepted and Tom was sentenced to death. In jail he gave several interviews and there is a famous photograph of him plaiting a horse-hair rope (claimed by some to be the one he was hanged with!). Tom Horn died game, but after his death there were many who believed that he had been innocent and was 'railroaded' to the gallows. Even today in certain parts of Wyoming, the name Tom Horn is certain to start arguments.

The bad men of the West came in all sorts and sizes, and all manner of temperaments, but their common denominator – the ability to kill without compunction if necessary – was augmented by one other trait: a healthy disregard for law and order and those who enforced it. But fortunately, as we shall see, there were men just as determined that they would abide by the law or perish.

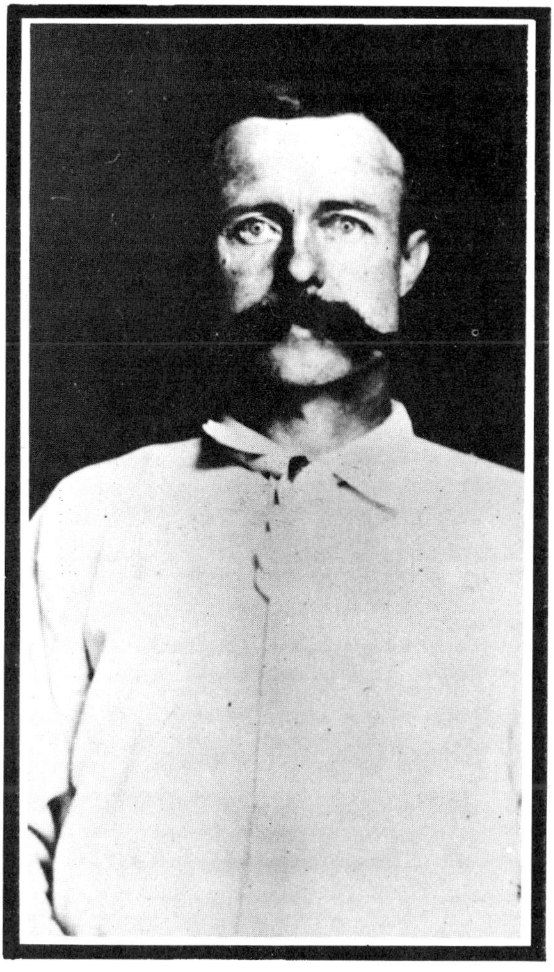

46
'Buckskin Frank' Leslie was a Tombstone badman, notable as a fast gun and a ladies man, and a menace when drunk. In 1880, he shot one Mike Killeen over the latter's wife, was cleared of homicide, then married the widow. She divorced him after seven years, though she had allegedly allowed him earlier to use her as a target, shooting bullets around her to 'draw' her profile. Later, he killed his common law wife, Mollie Bradshaw, and spent six years in Yuma penitentiary for the crime.

47
Westerners had an odd fascination for the macabre, hence the large number of 'morgue' photographs. Here is Ned Christie, a Cherokee who went to the bad as a bandit, horse-thief, whiskey runner and killer. For seven years he evaded capture in Indian Territory (later Oklahoma) before Chief Justice Parker's iron marshals caught up with him. It was claimed that he had gunned down nine men, one woman and a boy. He and two companions were finally caught in a log fort in the Spavinaw Hills. US marshals Heck Thomas and Paden Tolbert are alleged to have imported an army cannon and gone in with sixteen men. An estimated 2000 rifle slugs and thirty shells failed, so dynamite was used to blast out a side of the fort. Christie decided not to surrender and was shot down, Winchester in hand, the Winchester seen above.

48
The most famous group portrait in Western history, and one that was a great help to Pinkerton men when it was found. Here are the cream of the Wild Bunch, beautifully turned out, and taken by a Fort Worth photographer. From left to right, back row: Bill Carver and Harvey Logan. Front row: Harry Longabaugh (alias the Sundance Kid, after an exploit in Sundance, Wyoming), Ben 'The Tall Texan' Kilpatrick, Robert 'George' Leroy Parker, alias Butch Cassidy. Operating from remote hideouts in Wyoming and Utah, their career reached its climax with spectacular train robberies at the turn of the century, soon after which Butch and the Sundance Kid exited for Bolivia. For all its humour and (admittedly brilliant) directorial gimmicks, the movie Butch Cassidy and the Sundance Kid *gave a reasonably accurate account of the pair, not least the fact that Butch was remarkably non-violent by Western standards. It is now almost certain that they were not killed in Bolivia, but returned to the States, Butch's sister having convinced even sceptics that they came home. Ben Kilpatrick was killed in one of the last hold-ups of all in 1912. His reflexes had become slow and he was struck down by a guard with an ice mallet.*

49

The most famous posse to try and catch the Wild Bunch is pictured here in the special train provided for them (complete with horse stalls) by Union Pacific. From left to right are T. T. Keliher, H. Davis, George Hiatt, T. Jeff Carr (who once tangled with Wild Bill Hickok in Cheyenne and lived to tell the tale), Si Funk, and a man claimed to be Joe Lefors, who tricked Tom Horn into confessing his guilt over the Willie Nickell murder.

4 WESTWARD THE LAW

A few years ago a deputy marshal could travel anywhere unmolested, but now they have to go in squads for self-protection from bands of desperadoes roaming through the country, seeking persons to murder and plunder.
Western Independent,
Fort Smith, Arkansas, 21 August 1873

Early in the 1870s the mayor of a West Texas town sent the following telegram to the headquarters of the Texas Rangers at Austin: 'Have riot in town urgently need company of rangers'. Two days later, as the train from Austin clanked and spluttered to a halt at the depot, an eager crowd, led by the mayor, pressed forward to witness the Rangers' arrival.

50
Frederick Remington's 'Texas Ranger'.

Moments later, a tall, slim young man stepped down from the rear car and casually walked toward the crowd of people. He stopped, dropped his bag on the platform and carefully laid his Winchester rifle across it. He pushed his hat to the back of his head and opened his coat. His Colt was holstered high up on his hip and on his shirt front gleamed a silver star set in a silver circle – the badge of the Texas Rangers.

The mayor pushed forward. 'Where's the rest of 'em?' he asked anxiously.

'There's just me,' replied the young man.

'But I asked for a company,' croaked the mayor, desperation creeping into his voice.

'So you did,' smiled the young Ranger, 'but there's only one riot ain't there?'

That story, or versions of it, has delighted Texans and admirers of the Texas Rangers for almost a century, for the belief in 'one riot, one Ranger' was and is still a part of the mystique that surrounds the 'gentlemen in the white hats'.

But law and order out West was not always so readily available or as welcome.

The West of the early years of the nineteenth century was largely lawless. Walter Prescott Webb has even suggested that lawlessness in later periods existed because many of the laws were unsuited to the needs and conditions of the country. He reasoned that men could not abide by them and survive. Some of the laws were absurd and ignored local customs which should have been considered when implementing new laws. 'The blame for a great deal of Western lawlessness', he wrote in his classic *The Great Plains*, 'rests more with the lawmakers than with the lawbreaker.'

It was true that as civilisation spread westwards and adapted itself to the conditions of the country, so the law was adapted to suit the needs of the people. Where there was none at all the frontiersmen improvised. There is a story about Davy Crockett and a trek he made through the green forests of Tennessee. At a place called Shoal Creek he fell ill so decided to stay there. He soon realised that there was no law and order; but Davy felt that he 'could get along without order as well as anybody else'.

However, after about three years of lawlessness he and his neighbours finally took action. By that time all manner of bad characters had begun to flock into their community, so the residents set up a temporary form of government. Constables were selected and Crockett was appointed magistrate. In this manner they managed to keep some semblance of law and order until the State legislature took over the problem.

The early squatter courts, vigilantes and other forms of citizens' organisations to maintain some form of law and order, all based their concept on early English law. One famous incident occurred in May 1834, in what later became Iowa, when a man named Patrick O'Connor killed one George O'Keaf without provocation. The citizens got up a jury, elected counsel and put the man on trial. The jury found him guilty. Being responsible citizens they approached the governor of Missouri Territory for confirmation of the death sentence or a reprieve (Iowa had once been a part of that Territory). The governor could not help but suggested that they approach the President of the United States, Andrew Jackson. In his reply the President said that as the laws of the United States did not at that time extend to Iowa they must make their own decision. O'Connor was hanged.

Despite its apparent lawlessness, it was Texas that took the first steps towards establishing some form of law and order. In the mid 1820s the Mexicans, who then owned Texas, passed a colonisation law to encourage foreign immigrants, and the whites flocked to the area. Their major problem was the Plains Indians, notably the Comanches, who understandably resented the white man's arrival and harrassed him whenever possible. In May 1823, the Spanish governor agreed to the enlistment of a sergeant and fourteen men to help protect the settlers. They were poorly armed and equipped, but their presence was more than welcome. Later, Stephen F. Austin financed ten men out of his own pocket whom he called 'rangers', who later increased in numbers and reputation. But it was not until 1835 during the outbreak of the Texas Revolution against Mexico that the term 'Texas Rangers' came into general use, and it is that date which historians accept as the official origin of this world famous force.

Following the fall of the Alamo in 1836 to the Mexican dictator Santa Anna, and his subsequent defeat at San Jacinto shortly afterwards, the Texas Rangers became a regular part of the struggling Republic of Texas's efforts to establish law and order. Most of them were a rough-looking bunch, but when the war with Mexico broke out in 1846, they again proved their worth as a fighting force. They continued to protect the citizens when, following the end of the war in 1848, Texas became a state of the Union.

During the American Civil War the Rangers' activities are obscure. Even the Plains Indians in Texas seem to have been quiet, hoping perhaps that the whites would kill each other and save them the trouble. Both North and South did their best to placate the tribes and where possible enlist them into their service. Many Rangers enlisted into Confederate regiments, and those that remained in the Frontier force were thought by some uncharitable people to be 'dodgin' Injun arrows when they should've been dodgin' Yankee bullets!'

When the war ended in 1865, and the Indians once more began harrassing the settlers, it was suddenly realised that there were no longer any Texas Rangers. And the Federal Government was determined that there would not be. The idea of a semi-military force not controlled by the Union Army alarmed the 'Reconstructionists' among the military authorities governing Texas, and the argument that such a force was necessary to protect Frontier settlements from marauding Indians and Mexican cattle rustlers was dismissed as irrelevant. Besides, if the Indians did start trouble, the Union Army could take care of the situation. So Texas seethed first under the strict military control of the Army, and then reached boiling point when in 1869 F. J. Davis, a Republican, supported by the Union Army, was elected governor and took office in 1870.

Aware of the hatred against him in the state, the well-meaning but unwise Davis, to protect himself and his administration, appealed for a special force of militia to maintain law and order. And on 1 July 1870 the Texas State Police was organised, 157 men led by General James Davidson, bolstered by every local peace officer.

This formidable force was composed mostly of Negroes

but the officers were white. Encouraged by the protection of the Union Army and backed by the governor, all manner of crimes were laid at their door. Not all of the state police were corrupt, however, for some of the men who led them were ex-Rangers and they refused to become involved with the schemes of their superiors. But by 1873 the Texans had had enough. What good the state police did (and official records disclose that they did arrest a number of wanted horse-thieves, murderers and other criminals) was overshadowed by their actions against innocent people.

On 11 April 1873, the mouthpiece of the Davis administration, the *Daily State Journal* published a Roll of Honour of twelve policemen killed doing their duty. In reply the *Daily Democratic Statesman* on 17 April published a similar list of seventeen men murdered by the state police. By now the state legislature was controlled by the Democrats and a bill to repeal the police force was, despite a veto by the governor, passed on 22 April. The editor of the *State Gazette* claimed that the worst class of Negro had been enlisted, and 'sent forth to redress the imaginary grievances of their race'. For most people, however, it was the end of a nightmare. The same newspaper also published an apt epitaph to the Texas State Police: 'The police law is abolished over the Governor's veto. Glory to God in the highest; on earth, peace, good will towards men.'

It was then that some startling facts came to light. James Davidson had quit office in company with $34,000 of public funds and it was clear that others were probably involved. Davis's days, too, were numbered. He lost the November election and in his place as governor came Richard Coke who was quick to take note of the public's cry: 'Bring back the Rangers!'

With Coke's backing the legislature created two distinct forces of Texas Rangers: the Frontier Battalion, commanded by Major John B. Jones (who was responsible for the death of Sam Bass), and a Special Force of Rangers led by Captain L. H. McNally, a Civil War veteran and one of the few honourable ex-officers of the state police.

The Frontier Battalion was designed to control the Indians in the West, while the Special Force devoted itself to the suppression of banditry and cattle rustling on the Mexican Border. Thus it was that the Rangers helped law and order in Texas and in the process created the legend that even today brings a sense of relief and pride to Texans in trouble when they hear the cry: 'The Rangers are coming!'

Less well known, but highly effective between 1901 and 1909, were the Arizona Rangers under a dedicated, hard-bitten ex-cattleman, Captain Burton C. Mossman. The Arizona Territory, formed in 1862, had always been a haven for the lawless, and there were plenty left in the remoter regions at the turn of the century. Mossman and his fourteen men achieved marvels.

But for most other Frontier states and territories, law and order stemmed from local, state and Federal law, with occasional help from detective agencies, Pinkerton's being the most famous. Alan Pinkerton was born in Scotland in 1819 and was the son of a Glasgow police sergeant. He emigrated to Canada and later went to the States, where his genius as a detective rapidly became apparent. During the Civil War he was closely linked with the Secret Service and helped guard Abraham Lincoln. Later, he and his sons made their agency – 'We Never Sleep' was the motto – nationally famous. It was the most formidable opponent of the James Gang and helped put Butch Cassidy and the Wild Bunch out of business. The agency was the first to use 'mug shots' of wanted men, complete with descriptions of character and characteristics.

51
Allan Pinkerton, Scottish-born founder of the famous firm of detectives which tracked down bad men in the East as well as the Wild West.

Most famous of all in the fight against crime were the US marshals, legendary figures like the Texas Rangers and the North-West (later the Royal Canadian) Mounted Police. The undercover marshal has always been a Hollywood favourite. When all seems lost and Our Hero is about to be shot or hung as a 'darn rustlin' coyote' or some other anti-social being, the marshal somehow manages to produce his badge and enlist the lynch mob's aid in tracking down the real villains.

In reality, US marshals rarely became so involved with the public, leaving such duties to their deputies, who worked with local law enforcement agencies. The office of US marshal was created in 1789 and was a Presidential appointment confirmed by the Senate.

Marshals were given territories or states and allowed to appoint deputies. Until 1896 they did not have official commissions (although normally they were issued with a letter of authority) and were paid a fee instead of a salary. Since most of the men who were appointed deputy US marshals were already serving peace officers, the fees received were regarded as a supplement to their sometimes meagre pay as town marshal or county sheriff. The duties of a US marshal were principally concerned with Federal crimes, desertion from the Army, and crimes committed on Indian Reservations.

Perhaps the most publicised of all deputy US marshals were those employed by Judge Isaac Parker. Until he arrived at Fort Smith in the early 1870s virtually the whole of the area (Indian Territory, now the state of Oklahoma) was attached for judicial purposes to the United States Court for the Western District of Arkansas. However, it was not until the Judge arrived that any really effective measures were taken against the lawless element that infested the region. The Judge and his court became legendary, and the tenacity of his 'iron men' (as some called his deputies) in tracking down criminals was a byword. Many murderers came before the Judge and a number of them were hanged on the large multi-trap gallows built at the fort – in front of suitably impressed crowds. As time went by the Judge's 'empire' was whittled away until by 1896 it was gone, but law and order had arrived to stay.

52
Isaac Parker was dubbed the 'Hanging Judge' but few of his colleagues ever had to deal with so wild a territory as he.

Law and order, as has been shown, had always been a most pressing problem for the Western states. As more people flooded into states and territories the crock of gold at the end of most people's rainbow was land, and the more they could get their hands on the better. As wagons lumbered into sparsely populated areas and likely places were found that had plenty of water and timber, boundaries as such were either ignored or non-existent. Some settlers in the more remote areas had few problems, but as the land around the popular places

53
Judge Roy Bean, whose eccentric methods seem more amusing today than they can have been to his victims.

became densely populated (by their standards) there came the problem of staking a legal claim to their few acres. Those that ignored this basic safeguard soon found themselves ousted by claim jumpers. Various claim associations or tribunals sprang up to help protect them and from these came 'squatters courts'. Against such opposition many of the jumpers thought better of it and sought easier prey elsewhere.

Among the colourful characters who are remembered as early law-enforcers was Judge Roy Bean the 'Law West of the Pecos'. His shack-cum-saloon was situated in the small railroad town of Langtry on the edge of the Big Bend region of Texas, a mountainous wilderness that was a notorious hideout for outlaws. Bean fell in love with a picture of Lily Langtry, the actress mistress of King Edward VII (when he was Prince of Wales), known as 'the Jersey Lily' and named it after her. It was a most remarkable place overlorded by an equally remarkable man.

Bean hailed originally from Mason County, Kentucky, where he had been born in an obscure log cabin beside the Ohio river sometime during the 1820s. He led a hectic early life which had taken him as far as California, Arizona, New Mexico, and finally Texas. His frequent brushes with the law, both legally and illegally had given him an insight into its working and he quickly learned how to manipulate it for profit or against unscrupulous individuals.

In the early 1880s, having fallen out with his wife and neighbours, Bean gathered his belongings together and armed with a tent and some kegs of whiskey set out along the tracks of the Southern Pacific Railroad, and en route sold his whiskey to the hard-working, hard-drinking Irishmen of the construction crews. At Eagle's Nest on the banks of the Rio Grande he set up his tent and was soon doing a roaring trade selling food, cigars and whiskey. To the men working the tracks it was like an oasis and Bean's 'place' was a great attraction.

With the Irishmen were Chinese and others who found difficulty in communication. Added to this was the inevitable racial prejudice, and, once tension reached breaking point, Bean was frequently embroiled in their fights. Yet it proved to be the making of him. His knowledge of the law was considerably greater than his actual schooling in it and the three 'r's', and this, combined with his 'judgelike' bearing, his acknowledged dexterity with a six-shooter and coolness in handling troublemakers, soon commanded the respect not only of his customers but also of his neighbours.

Travellers coming in from the desert or stretching their legs as the trains stopped for water or fuel, were eager to catch up on the latest shootings in the area. One young lady went up to the 'judge' and timidly asked him why it was so quiet – hadn't she heard that it was a wild place? Bean drew himself up to his full height, stared soberly at her, and gravely shook his head. 'Ma'am, everything's perfectly peaceful here – why we ain't had a killin' for at least four hours!'

When it was learned that there was no court nearer than Fort Stockton, almost 200 miles away, the Texas Rangers stationed at Eagle's Nest occasionally brought in prisoners for Bean to judge. He had no real jurisdiction, except perhaps 'common consent' backed by Ranger pistols, but the Rangers soon rectified that. Roy Bean was appointed justice of the peace on 2 August 1882. It took him some months to find his $6000 bond, but nobody worried too much about that. The important thing was that the law had finally come 'West of the Pecos'.

From Eagle's Nest Bean's 'court' later moved to Vinegaroon, where he further enhanced his reputation by fining those who answered him back during court exchanges – few offenders dared question his verdict after that! A couple of moves later he was settled in what was subsequently to be-

54
Black Bart, who robbed Wells Fargo stage coaches and got away with thousands of dollars before he was tracked down by the company's famous investigator James B. Hume. Black Bart, whose real name was Charles E. Bolton, never killed anyone, and was noted particularly for his poetry and delighted in signing himself 'Black Bart the PO8'.

come Langtry, and the now world famous sign 'Judge Roy Bean Notary Public. Justice of the Peace. Law West of the Pecos. Ice Beer' was erected.

One of Bean's notorious rulings would today be classified as extreme racialism. A Chinese railroad hand was killed in a brawl in 1884, and the accused, an Irishman, appeared in court accompanied by a band of husky companions. Ben was made to understand that the wrong verdict might prove disastrous to his business and damaging to his health. Perplexed, the judge thumbed through his 'statoot' book, and after some moments of deliberation, stabbed his finger on a page and glared around the court. 'Gents,' he boomed out, 'this here court finds that the law is explicit on the killin' of a fellow man, but there ain't nothin' about knockin' off a heathen Chinee – case dismissed! And the drinks is on Paddy there!'

Today the Judge Roy Beans of the Old West are often regarded as comic figures, but at the time when they were the only law available – outrageous and perhaps 'unlawful' though it sometimes was – ordinary people were grateful that at least there was someone they could turn to.

A character in the same vein as Bean was Marcellus E. Joyce, an Irish journalist who came to Hays City, Kansas, in October 1867, ostensibly to cover the arrival of the Union Pacific Eastern Division Railway for the Leavenworth *Commercial*. He liked the place so much that he resigned from the paper and was later appointed justice of the peace. Joyce was a short, sandy-haired individual with a large red handlebar mustache. Scrupulously honest in his legal dealings, he nonetheless had a great sense of humour.

Writing in the Topeka *State Journal* in 1890, Colonel Henry Inman recalled how the little Irishman conducted his court. On one occasion a fellow Irishman appeared before him for some misdemeanor and he fined him $40. To his disgust the man told him he had no money. Joyce pondered a while. He did not wish to send the fellow to jail but he wanted money from somewhere. Someone told him that the defendant's brother, newly arrived from Ireland, was in court, and the judged ordered him before him.

'Do you have any cash?' he asked.

'I sure do, your honour!'

'Well, then me bucky – the fine's on you!'

A cowboy was brought before Joyce accused of murder, and legend has it that a sum of $500 was slipped to the judge prior to the trial. When the accused was asked if he pleaded guilty or not guilty, he foolishly answered 'guilty'. 'Well,' retorted the judge, 'yees are a big fool to plade that way, and I discharge yees for want of ividence!'

Old-timers recall that Joyce's court and brand of justice was always a topic of conversation. Some even alleged that he was known on occasion to dispense with his signature and byline 'Notary Public' and write instead 'Notorious Public!' But Joyce actually took his job very seriously and his reputation as a humourist was greatly exaggerated.

The closer people got to civilised communities and townships, so did the law gradually resemble the accepted version now a familiar part of everyday life. As we shall see, its presence in the cowtowns was frequently a contest between the itinerant cowboys and others who were passing through, and the elected town marshals and police imported or locally elected to control them. This situation was particularly acute in the mining towns.

California set the pattern, which was to vary little until the Mounties brought their own matchless brand of law and order to the Klondike. Except for the first idyllic summer of 1848 in California, when there was gold for almost everyone, crime and violence flourished mightily. At a time when every rumour of gold sent men rushing deeper into the wilderness – a recurring pattern all over the West – law and order in terms of lawmen and judges was almost non-existent in new mining 'towns', big or small.

Robberies proliferated, tempers frayed, and as jails were conspicuous by their absence, men often took the law into their own hands without even bothering with the by no means difficult formalities of organising vigilance committees.

Standard punishments were death, whipping, or banishment from the fields, and the most regular victims were foreigners, especially Chinese. (Native Californian Indians were almost exterminated.)

One of the most vivid descriptions of Lynch law in action

1

2

1
Wild Bill Hickok walked the streets of the cowtowns dressed like a New York fashion plate. But 'the dandy was deadly' as many learned to their cost. From an original painting by Richard Scollins.

2
'Gunfight' by N. C. Wyeth.

3
'In Without Knocking' by Charles M. Russell.

3

4

4

The Civil War proved the worth of the percussion revolver. Left is an 1851 Model Colt 'Navy' typical of those which saw service in the bloody Kansas-Missouri Border wars and later the Civil War. Shown cocked is an 1860 'Army' revolver manufactured in 1863 that was used in the latter stages of the Civil War. Included are some .44 lead balls for the Army and a lead-backed Union Army cross strap buckle.

5a

The Williamson derringer. First manufactured in 1866, these sleek-looking pistols are only 5in long. Made in .36 and .41 calibres it is a dual ignition weapon – that is, it can fire a rim-fire cartridge or, by means of a metal insert, loose powder and ball.

b

A small catch beneath the stock releases the barrel so that it slides forward to load either a cartridge or the powder container shown above the pistol. A percussion cap is placed upon the nipple at the rear, and the hammer is designed to ignite either system.

5a

b

MARSHAL
DEADWOOD
REWARD!
WELLS, FARGO & CO'S
Express was Robbed this Morning, between Ione Valley and Galt, by two men, described as follows:
One elderly, heavy set, and sandy complexion. The other tall, slim, and dark complexion.
$200 Each and one-fourth
the Treasure recovered, will be
d for the arrest and conviction
he robbers.
JNO. J. VALENTINE, Gen. Supt.
May 3d, 1875.

6

The changing West. Shown on the left, flanking a Wells Fargo Reward poster, is a nickel-plated ivory-butted Colt 1873 Model 'Peacemaker' surrounded by its ammunition and three typical lawmen's badges. At the top is a town marshal's badge from Deadwood, and below it a more modern sheriff's badge issued by Atchison County, Kansas. Beneath the two is a deputy US marshal's badge. The gunbelt is circa 1880, and the spur came from Dodge City, Kansas, where, it is alleged, it was removed from a horsethief lynched in 1872. The items shown at the right are associated with Civil War and postwar Cavalry and civilian use. At the top is a plain belt with a reverse-draw flap holster. The buckle is the type introduced in 1851 which remained in use until the early 1870s when it was replaced by the bronze version shown below. The Colt .44 calibre 1860 'Army' revolver was used by the military and some gunfighters, but many of them, including cowboys, preferred the lighter .36 calibre 1851 'Navy' shown with a typical hand-carved reverse-draw holster. Included are some .44 calibre lead balls, a 7th Cavalry cross sabres cap badge and a lead-backed Civil War cross belt buckle.

7
Some historic Colts. Top left: the 1848 Model 'Dragoon'. Below: an 1851 Model 'Navy'. Bottom: the 1877 Model double-action 'Lightning'. Top right: the 1860 New Model 'Army'. Below: a nickel-plated ivory-butted single-action 'Army' revolver Model 1873, commonly called the 'Peacemaker'. The pistol pictured here came from Dodge City where it was once owned by a member of the town's police force.

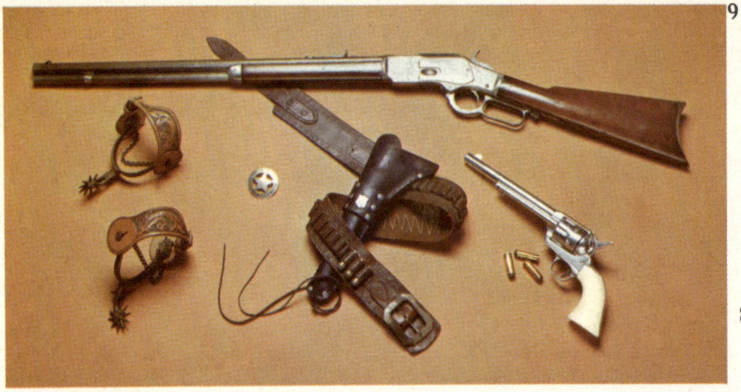

8
'The Hold-Up' by Charles M. Russell.

9
Most lawmen travelled light, and their equipment was restricted to essentials. At the top is the famous Winchester rifle, model of 1873, and below it a nickel-plated ivory-butted Colt 1873 'Peacemaker' manufactured in 1875. The holster is modern, but is typical of the time, while the belt was made in the early 1880s. Included is a marshal's star, and a pair of Texas spurs made in the 1880s, but fitted with modern hand-carved leathers.

10
'The Deadman's Hand'. This poker hand – Aces of Clubs and Spades; two black eights, Clubs and Spades, and the Jack of Diamonds – was held by Wild Bill when he was murdered in Deadwood. Also illustrated are a .36 calibre Colt 'Navy', a key-wind Swiss watch made in the 1860s; a silver dollar dated 1882, and an ivory poker chip that came from the Long Branch saloon, Dodge City.

11
Left: An early Henry .44 rimfire lever-action rifle, the forerunner of the 1866 Winchester. These weapons were first used in limited numbers during the Civil War, and later were popular on the Plains. Right: The Winchester rifle, Model 1892. Popular in various calibres, it is best known in .30-30 calibre. The '92 is the Winchester most frequently used in Western films – even when the action takes places years before it was invented!

55
The famous photograph of Judge Roy Bean presiding over his 'court', complete with hat and holstered pistol. He could not spell his beloved 'Jersey Lily' correctly.

in a mining area occurs in Edward Buffum's *The Gold Rush* (1850). Buffum, a former journalist and volunteer soldier, was at the Old Day Diggings in 1849 when five men were caught in the act of robbing a gambler. After thirty-nine lashes apiece, three of them, two French and one Chilean, none of whom spoke English, were also accused of attempted armed robbery and murder some months earlier. Within half an hour 200 'jurors' had sentenced them to hang, and hang they did despite Buffum's valiant intervention:

I mounted a stump and in the name of God, humanity, and law, protested against such a course of proceeding; but the crowd, by this time excited by frequent and deep potations of liquor from a neighbouring groggery, would listen to nothing contrary to their brutal desires, and even threatened to hang me if I did not immediately desist from any further remarks.

Buffum gave up and prepared to watch the 'horrible tragedy'. The men were given half an hour to prepare themselves, but tried to plead as the ropes were put round their necks:

They vainly tried to speak, but none of them understanding English, they were obliged to use their native tongues . . . Vainly they called for an interpreter, for their cries were drowned by the yells of the now infuriated mob . . . at a given signal, without priest or prayer book, the wagon was drawn from under them, and they were launched into eternity.

Long after mining camps turned into towns - Virginia City, Deadwood, Tombstone and other less fabled spots – the lure of gold and silver ensured that they remained more than somewhat lively. Though Virginia City, Nevada, reached its peak of productivity in the seventies, when its name rang round the world, it was booming in the early sixties when Mark Twain was a newspaperman there. As he noted in *Roughing It*:

There were military companies, fire companies, brass bands, banks, hotels, theatres, 'hurdy-gurdy houses', wide-open gambling palaces, political pow-wows, civic processions, street fights, murders, inquests, riots, a whisky mill every fifteen steps . . . a dozen breweries and half a dozen jails and station houses in full operation, and some talk of building a church.

In other words, law and order had at least raised its head there, more than at Last Chance Gulch (later Helena), Montana, where in 1864 we are told, 'the crack of the revolver was often heard above the merry notes of the violin . . . Pistols flashed bowie knives flourished, and oaths filled the air.'

The corruption that blossomed where gold was found meant that such lawmen as there were might be in the pay of the lawless, though, as already related, Henry Plummer managed to combine the job of master criminal and sheriff with astonishing success for a time. But for sheer outrageous sin, 'Soapy' Smith of Skagway ill-fame takes the prize for making the most of a mining situation.

'Soapy', a con man extraordinary, made his name and earned his nickname in Denver, Colorado, by convincing miners and others that the five dollar shaving-soap sticks that he sold might have dollar bills under their wrappers. The first stick usually had a hundred dollar bill, nearly all the rest were pure soap.

Like the rest of the world, 'Soapy' heard about the fabulous gold strike in the Klondike on Canadian Territory. It was made in August 1896 and news – so remote was the area – broke in July 1897 when two boatloads of Bonanza Kings reached Seattle and San Francisco. The world promptly suffered its last great bout of gold fever.

The Stampeders who reached Dawson in the heart of the mining area in 1898, after journeys by various routes which ranged from rugged to nightmarish, found the fields policed by Superintendent Sam Steele, 'the Lion of the Yukon', and a handful of men of the North-West Mounted Police. Such were their qualities that law and order reigned – though plenty of liveliness was allowed – and in 1898 there was not a single killing in Dawson and robberies were rarities.

Things could not have been more different in Skagway, Alaska on American Territory, where 'Soapy' Smith controlled the town in a manner beyond the wildest dreams of even a Hollywood scriptwriter.

Skagway was the key place on the least terrible route to the Klondike. Ships landed stampeders there, who then had to trek across one of two alarming passes, the White or Chilkoot.

Few would-be miners got through Skagway without falling into the clutches of 'Soapy' and his gang. He controlled the law, places of entertainment, the carriers on the passes and the roads to them. The Mounties would not allow anyone into the Klondike without a year's supplies – to prevent famine – so it required several journeys to get past the top. 'Soapy' and his men never got into the Klondike, but they made a killing on the way up.

Many stampeders never got out of Skagway, for the gang had ways of fleecing new arrivals of all their money and possessions. They sensibly did not fleece the townspeople, but gradually the stench created by his methods, and the continuous sound of six-guns in Skagway, shamed the inhabitants to follow the lead of one Frank Reid.

'Soapy' Smith had guts, for in the final crisis he went out to the hostile crowd with a derringer in his sleeve, a .45 Colt in his pocket and a Winchester over his shoulder to 'teach these damned sons of bitches a lesson', while some of his gang melted away to the hills. He came face to face with Reid near the dock and levelled the Winchester at his head. Reid grabbed the muzzle and pulled it downwards, reaching for his pistol with his right hand. As Smith shouted: 'Don't shoot!', Reid fired, but the cartridge was faulty. Smith's Winchester sent a bullet into his groin, then both men fired again and a bullet in his heart ended 'Soapy' Smith's reign of terror. The mortally wounded Reid exulted before he died: 'I got the sonofabitch. He may have got me, boys, but by God I got him first!' As for the gang, amazingly they were not lynched, those that were caught merely being jailed. Times were changing.

The 'Boom Town' effect of the gold rush era was repeated in the cowtowns, but unlike the mining camps, the majority of the cowtowns were either established before the arrival of the cattle or outlived the trade. Few mining camps could claim that.

In establishing law and order in cowtowns like Abilene, Wichita and Dodge City, local communities had to contend with opposition both from the people the marshals were employed to protect and from

56

In May 1884, the bank at Medicine Lodge, Kansas, was held up by a gang who killed the president and the cashier. The gang escaped, only to be captured by a posse. To the amazement of all, the gang's leader turned out to be Henry Newton Brown, marshal of Caldwell, together with his assistant, Ben Wheeler, both of whom had recently been given guns in appreciation for services rendered. The captives were jailed in Medicine Lodge, but a mob invaded the jail during the night and overpowered the sheriff and his deputies. There was a scuffle and shots were fired, during which the prisoners tried to escape. Wheeler was badly wounded and quickly recaptured along with two others. Brown got away, but was tracked down and killed by a charge of buckshot and several bullets. Despite their protests, Wheeler and his companions were lynched. The photograph shows the gang when first captured. From left to right: John Wesley, Henry Newton Brown, Billy Smith and Ben Wheeler.

those they were hired to control. Some citizens, whose financial interests might be affected if too many restrictions were placed upon their customers, fought against local legislation, but mostly they were overruled. Either way the police had a tough time. Most of them were hard-headed realists who regarded their job as a means of earning a living and not a vocation. The pay was not high, except in a few instances, but it was regular, and with a good force to back them up most town marshals were confident they could keep the peace.

Hollywood has dominated the Western scene for so long that few people now appreciate that the lone man so popular in Westerns is a mythical creation who in real life did not exist. *High Noon* was a great Western, but it was historically inaccurate – in real life Gary Cooper's Marshal Will Kane would have had no trouble in gaining public support in his fight against the Miller gang.

Each American state is divided up into counties, and in charge of the law enforcement for the county is a sheriff – something the United States also inherited from the English legal system. Normally a sheriff is elected to office for two years. Most men in this position are politically ambitious, and the same could be said for their Old West counterparts. A sheriff rarely had much to do with criminals at large personally, and he left much of the routine work to his under sheriff and deputies. The old-time sheriffs were paid from about $200 to perhaps $500 (which was exceptional) per month, their salaries largely dependant on how rich the county was or how much the County Commissioners were prepared to pay. The under sheriff got approximately half of the sheriff's salary, and the deputies about two-thirds of the under sheriff's salary, so apart from the top job law enforcement was rarely well paid.

One of the deputy sheriffs (most sheriffs had two) was employed as county jailer, and if there was any need for extra assistance special deputies were sworn in. While the sheriff and his staff took care of county matters, the local police looked after cities, and again a similar situation applied.

Each town had its marshal or Chief of Police, and he in turn had as many deputies or 'policemen' as the town council thought necessary. A typical cowtown had two or possibly three policemen besides the marshal, but when the season got started others might be hired for various duties, such as keeping an eye on dance halls, brothels and theatres. Police records were kept up-to-date by the marshal, and it was his responsibility to see that numerous mundane tasks were also taken care of. These included traffic duty, the removal of obstructions, repairs to the roads and sidewalks, sweeping the streets and keeping an eye on blocked flues or chimneys. It was not uncommon to see prisoners from the local jail either under guard or shackled together while they worked at such tasks. It was very much a routine existence, and for most town marshals the only target practice they got, apart from the occasional shoot-out, was the dubious pleasure of shooting stray dogs for a small fee.

57
The Medicine Lodge posse.

If things did get too tough for his meagre force, a marshal could rely upon the citizens to come to his aid. This action was rarely called for, but the continuous ringing of the fire alarm or the police bell soon brought armed men running to assist.

Police officers, marshals and sheriffs came from all classes of society. Very few were professionals, but some who remained in office any length of time invariably became experts in their chosen vocation. For the most part, however, cowtown police were transients who remained in office sometimes only for a few months. Those who stayed longer were exceptional. They were employed because they were considered to be equal to the task; men whose courage and known ability with a gun was regarded as superior to the majority of those whom they were expected to control. Against such men, now immortalised in legend as 'two gun marshals', was a whole host of characters, the most colourful and unpredictable of all was the Texas cowboy.

5 CATTLE, COWBOYS AND COWTOWNS

His diet is principally Navy plug and whisky, and the occupation of his heart is gambling . . . He generally wears a revolver on each side, which he will use with as little hesitation on a man as on a wild animal. Such a character is dangerous and desperate, and each one generally has killed his man.

Topeka *Daily Commonwealth,* 15 August 1871

One day in 1874, as a Kansas Pacific train clattered westwards across the tracks, the conductor approached a young cowboy slouched in the corner of his seat gloomily staring out at the vast expanse of flat Kansas grassland.

'Where's your ticket, son?' the conductor asked.

'Ain't got one,' was the surly reply.

'Well, then, how far y'-goin'?'

'To hell, I reckon,' growled the cowboy.

'Well, son,' grinned the conductor, 'give me a dollar and get off at Dodge City!'

Such was the reputation of Dodge City and the other cowtowns dotted around parts of Kansas in the two decades following the Civil War that today it is hard to get beyond the myth and find the real story of these lively and fascinating outposts of 'civilisation' on the prairie.

It was, of course, the Texas cattle industry that gave them life, sustained them and eventually forsook them. Today some of those places are just a memory while others still bask in their former glory.

Some said you could smell it five miles away, and if not then the dust cloud would be enough. And the nearer it got the easier it became to smell, see and hear a herd of bellowing Texas longhorns-like an army on the march.

As the herd drew nearer riders detached themselves from the dust cloud and galloped towards the waiting shipping pens and the buyers. Already it was known whose herd was coming in, and both buyer and seller were anxious to complete the transaction and get the herd on board the waiting cattle trains and away to St Louis or Chicago for slaughter.

Driving a cattle herd to market was both dangerous and frustrating. The animals could not be rushed, and the long trek up from Texas was hazardous for man and beast; sometimes it took three months, by which time both animals and men had had enough. The main route came up via the Rio Grande river, on across Indian Territory (now Oklahoma) and up to Wichita. This was called the Chisholm Trail and was named after Jesse Chisholm, a half-Scots, half-Cherokee trader. From Wichita the trail branched off in various directions, and the part of it that extended to Abilene was called 'McCoy's Extension' or the 'Abilene Trail'. There were other trails, notably the Shawnee Trail which went as far as Kansas City and St Louis, and the Western Trail which ran from Fort Griffin up through the (Indian) Nations to Dodge City. But whatever the route, the cattle over the years had pounded it to a hard mud-packed road sometimes as large as four hundred yards wide.

Once the herds reached the railhead town they then had to wait their turn at the shipping pens and the opportunity was taken to fatten them up a little before shipment. Usually the herd was held several miles away at a place where there was plenty of water and grass. But once in town no time was lost in driving them to the pens to await the final journey by cattle car to market. Sometimes the cattle buyers then hired drovers to take their cattle on overland to places as far away as California, by which time the poor beasts had practically walked from one end of the United States to the other.

The creature that made the whole venture possible, the Texas longhorn, was a wild, mean, unpredictable animal, used to a free range, and most of them had grown to maturity without seeing a man. Consequently they were wary of them. Particularly dangerous were the full-grown bulls whose dispositions at any time were suspect. Early post-Civil War drives had been composed mostly of really wild animals, but later when drives were properly planned, the young bulls were castrated, and as 'steers' (maimed but untamed) they were headed north.

The longhorns became used to men on horseback, but once the pair parted company there could be trouble. Because of this where possible the pens were always situated well away from the main thoroughfares of any town so that most of the residents rarely saw them; but they were constantly reminded of their existence by the noise and the smell that drifted up town on the breeze.

As remarkable as the cattle were the men who rounded them up, branded them and finally drove them to market – the cowboys. Curiously, the word 'cowboy' has not always had such an obvious meaning. During the Revolutionary War bands of plunderers were employed by the British to bring in supplies, which included meat, and these men were known as 'cowboys'. Local farmers thought as little about shooting a cowboy as they did a wild animal or an Indian. Most of these characters were active in the New York area.

But the origin of the word so far as the Texas cattle industry is concerned is less involved. The Spanish word *vaquero*, or cowherd, continued in use long after the Texas cowboy became a familiar figure. None the less, as late as the early 1880s 'cowboy' was still used in a derogatory sense to indicate rustler or thief. Buffalo Bill's Wild West show changed the image when Buck Taylor (William Levi Taylor) was introduced to audiences as 'The King of the Cowboys', a title that has outlived even the Wild West show days and was used to describe the celluloid heroics of a number of Hollywood cowboy stars. Taylor led a band of devoted 'cowboy' followers around the arena pacifying hostile Indians and rescu-

58
A cattle stampede usually meant death on the prairie. Sometimes it was the longhorns which died, but all too often it was a cowboy, whose horse happened to step in a gopher hole and throw them both in the face of a thundering herd. His companions buried what was left of him in a solitary grave 'on the lone prairie'.

ing distressed maidens from 'a fate worse than death'. The dime novel played up the image and eventually the word 'cowboy' assumed heroic proportions.

In Kansas, however, the word 'cowboy' was almost unheard of until the early 1870s. The men who herded the cattle to the railheads were generally known as 'stockmen' or 'drovers' (the latter often applied to the herd owners) and occasionally just simply as 'the Texans'. In the early years following the Civil War most of them were white, but their ranks included a number of Mexican *vaqueros*. Later they were joined by Negroes until by the end of the century cowboys were multi-racial.

Colonel Richard Irving Dodge, in his book *Our Wild Indians: Thirty-Three Years' Personal Experience among the Red Men of the Great West*, wrote of the cowboy:

59
When the Texans first headed north to Kansas in 1866, they met opposition from farmers who complained that longhorns not only frightened domestic cattle, but infected them with the dreaded 'Texas fever'. Particularly violent were bands of ex-Civil War guerrillas who preyed on the cattlemen. Some they captured, tied up and whipped, then freed on payment of a 'toll' (some or all of their herd); but some were simply killed and their herds stolen. Only when Texans began using the Chisholm and other trails in growing numbers were they safe from such vicious attacks.

60
The scowling cowboy in the foreground of this evocative picture, complete with his pointing rifle, typifies the image expected of him and his friends. In less than serious vein, the man on the wagon pointing his gun at the seated figure is almost comic. This mealtime glimpse of a cow camp shows one of the few times that cowboys were able to relax.

For fidelity to duty, for promptness and vigor of action, for resources in difficulty, and unshaken courage in danger, the cowboy has no superior among men.

But there is something in this peculiar life which develops not only the highest virtues, but the most ignoble of vices. It is not solitude, for the shepherds of the Plains lead lives quite solitary, and they are generally quiet, inoffensive persons. The cowboy, on the contrary, is usually the most reckless of all the reckless desperadoes developed on the frontier. Disregarding equally the rights and lives of others, and utterly reckless of his own life; always ready with his weapons and spoiling for a fight, he is the terror of all who come near him, his visits to the frontier towns of Kansas and Nebraska being regarded as a calamity second only to a western tornado. His idea of enjoyment is to fill himself full of bad whiskey, mount his mustang, tear through the streets, whooping, yelling, flourishing and firing his pistols until the streets are deserted and every house closed, then with a grim smile of happiness he dashes off to his comrades to excite their envy by graphic pictures of his own exploits and the terror of the timid townspeople.

Others recalled that considering the life he led, the bad food he ate and the rigours of a semi-nomadic existence, unsociable hours, and little feminine company the cowboy deserved to let off steam on occasions. The ideal location was always the cowtown, the end of the drive.

The man who helped make all that possible was Joseph G. McCoy, no stranger to the cattle trade. For years the business had been expanding, but the outbreak of the American Civil War put an end to it. McCoy and his brothers had become well established in the business by that time and when the war ended sought to reopen their trade. Well aware of the many thousands of Texas cattle running loose in the brush country of Texas while their owners had been away fighting in the war, McCoy began negotiations with various railroads to set up a shipping point. In 1867, following talks with the Union Pacific Eastern Division Railway, and despite rigorous quarantine laws which barred Texas cattle from most parts of the state of Kansas for much of the year, he found a market at what was to become perhaps the most famous of all the cattle shipping points, Abilene, then a small hamlet far out on the tracks of the UPED.

Within months this 'small dead place' which boasted one saloon and a thriving prairie dog colony in the main street, had been transformed into a growing community. A large siding or 'switch' was built by the railroad to take one hundred cattle cars at one time. Huge pens and holding corrals were also erected, and on 5 September 1867, the first shipment of cattle left for Chicago.

61
A woodcut showing cowboys at Abilene. Note the way their pistols are carried – in the back of their belts, and usually with the butts facing forward.

Today the Kansas Cowtown is very much a part of the Western legend. Most of them followed the same layout. The railroad ran right through the middle of it, and acted as both a barrier between the business and residential sections and the line beyond which the cowboys did not go unless they were looking for trouble. On the 'wrong side of the tracks', as the respectable citizens disdainfully described the Texan half of Abilene, Wichita, Ellsworth, Caldwell or even Dodge City, were the brothels, gambling dens and saloons, together with various dance halls – sometimes a combination of all three.

Here the cowboy could revel to his heart's delight, and there were plenty ready to oblige him, card sharps, pimps, and prostitutes in particular. Many of the cowboys were unused to being around women and after a few drinks, and the prospect of a 'genital collision' inspired by whiffs of heady perfumes which the girls soaked themselves in, they eagerly entered the 'cribs' (spurs and all!) to prove their manhood. They returned home broke and proud even though, as often happened, in the fullness of time those careless moments of ecstasy left them with an unpleasant reminder.

A cowboy earned between thirty and forty dollars a month, and unless he lodged some of it

62
This wood engraving from a photograph made in Abilene in 1870 or 1871 first appeared in Joseph McCoy's Historic Sketches of the Cattle Trade of the West and Southwest, *published in 1874, and shows a typical cattle train passing in front of his celebrated Drover's Cottage.*

63
The stockyards at Abilene, from a photograph by Alexander Gardner in 1867.

with his boss for safe-keeping, he blew the lot in his mad gallop around the saloons, brothels and gambling halls (or 'hells') of the cowtowns. His trail-worn, verminous clothing was discarded in favour of new suits, boots and the inevitable 'ten gallon' stetson, for after so long on the trail he needed to relax, to let off steam and generally have a good time.

The town councils and the other citizens viewed these goings on with mixed feelings. Businessmen welcomed the transient custom and gleefully totted up their profits, as did the saloon men and others. Some advocated a complete stoppage of such activities, but it was pointed out that no entertainment at all would only bring trouble. So other means were devised to placate the sober citizens and at the same time enhance the city's wealth. Since many of the activities going on in the various 'establishments' were termed illegal according to various state and Federal laws, the city fathers imposed fines for offences against ordinances and the law, and so the Red Light districts payed large contributions to the city coffers.

Despite the obvious evils associated with the cattle trade its economic potential was enormous. Cattle driven up from Texas where they might sell for $8 to $10 a head could be sold for much more. One Texan

64
'Dressing up' was an essential part of a cowboy's relaxation when he hit town at the end of a long cattle drive. These three typical Texans were photographed in 1871 at the end of a drive. The man in the middle is J. H. Clements, a relative of John Wesley Hardin.

65
Isom Dart, a black outlaw, poses in a traditional manner against a studio backdrop. Round his waist is a narrow cartridge belt into which he has thrust a .44 Remington percussion revolver and what looks like a Belgian or French target pistol; both probably supplied by the photographer. Evidently the original of this photograph was a tintype, for it is printed in reverse.

66
Cowboy fashions did not change much in the 1870s and 1880s. Here James M Kellerman poses in Denver in 1885 dressed in conventional chaps, kneckerchief, broad-brimmed hat, rawhide quirt in hand, gauntlets and the inevitable six-shooter. Note how the holster covers all but the butt, and that it is worn high on the hip, supported by a narrow cartridge belt, the opposite of today's theatrical model cowboy.

drove a herd of 600 to Abilene in 1868 valued at about \$10 a head and sold them for \$16,800, assessing his actual expenses at \$4 per head – or \$9000 profit! Small wonder that the trade attracted such a variety of people.

We have seen that not all the cattle were shipped out by rail, for a large proportion were driven onwards overland to other markets. Some idea of how the cattle were distributed around the country can be gleaned from Joseph G. McCoy's *Historic Sketches of the Cattle Trade* published in 1874. He noted that driving cattle northwards from Abilene became quite as usual as driving up from Texas. He estimated that in 1871 190,000 head of cattle were sold at Abilene of which only 40,000 went by rail (the numbers were actually much higher). Other places had similar figures to report, and as late as 1882 the Dodge City *Globe* noted that 200,000 head had been bought and sold in the town, but of this number only about 65,000 had been shipped by rail. None the less, a cursory glance at the Kansas press for the period does show an active interest in the freighting of cattle by rail, from which the railroad reaped quite a profit.

Despite the obvious dangers and other evils of the trade, there was no shortage of would-be cowtowns in Kansas. Once it became known that the first

67
Primitive but very deadly. Wichita, Kansas, about 1870, looking north on what was to become Main Street from Douglas Avenue.

shipment of cattle had left Abilene for Chicago in 1867, and that she was asserting herself as the major shipping point, other places vied to get into the act. In August 1869, the Lawrence, Kansas, *Tribune* noted that 40,000 head of Texas cattle were awaiting shipment at Abilene and Salina, and that another 35,000 were on their way to both places. On the 11th the Leavenworth *Times and Conservative* said that: 'West of Eldorado, thirty miles, is the town of Wichita, a small military post and a small town. And this too is a Texas cattle trading point. Thousands of head of cattle are here, for sale, and many more are being sold in spite of the laws.'

The laws were the quarantine laws which barred Texas cattle from most parts of Kansas for much of the year. Fears of 'Spanish fever' a disease carried by ticks, and its effect on domestic stock had led to many problems and some violence by farmers to keep the longhorns out, so the only way the cattle could be moved through the settled regions was by rail.

Newton's period as a cowtown was relatively short, and by the time Abilene dropped out of the market it was Ellsworth that took over most of her business, and remained the principal cattle town until she was rivalled by Wichita. The first shipment of cattle by rail from Wichita left the town on 8 June 1872, barely a month after the railroad had reached the place. Eighteen cars left on the first train and two days later another twenty cars had clattered away to Chicago.

The next place to become a cattle shipping point of note was the one that today (apart

68
Ellsworth, Kansas, in 1867, photographed by Alexander Gardner.

from Abilene) is the best known – Dodge City, the self-styled 'Queen of the Cowtowns'. Founded in July 1872, the place was originally called Buffalo City, and was located five miles from Fort Dodge. From then until 1885 it reigned supreme as the major shipping point for Texas cattle despite a brief rivalry from Brookville and later Caldwell, which got into the cattle business rather late.

By 1885, however, the Kansas State Legislature had passed a law banning the trail-cattle industry, and but for a very few exceptions no more cattle came up the trails from Texas. It was the end of an era, and might well have passed into history but for the epic quality of the cattle-driving days and the violent men and women who gave it life and an immortality all of its own. So next we will look more closely at some of those people whose antics made it necessary to bring in gunfighting peace officers to control them.

69
Dodge City's Front Street in 1879, showing the famous 'Dodge House'.

70
Front Street, Dodge City, Kansas, in 1878. In the foreground are the tracks of the Santa Fe Railway. In the rear near the 'Dry Goods' store is the famous Long Branch Saloon, scene of several gunfights.

6 THE SALOON AND GAMBLING SET

Here, in a well-lighted room opening on the street the boys gather in crowds around the tables to play or to watch others play . . . The musicians had to compete with clinking glasses, jangling spurs, ribald shouts, laughter, and the occasional bark of a six-shooter.

Junction City *Weekly Union*, 29 October 1870, of the Alamo Saloon, Abilene

The saloon is the centre of attraction in most Western films or books, for here is the meeting place between good and evil; a place where men come to relax, to talk, and sometimes to die. It is here, too, that the hero, whose first entrance is greeted by a sudden silence, has to prove himself the equal of all comers, and where he meets the villain who has the town under his control; and it is in the saloon or immediately outside it that the pair fight their last fight.

In reality things were not quite like that, but the saloon was certainly the meeting place for most people, the social centre of a cowtown. To most men straight off the trail, or arriving in town from a hard trek or stagecoach, horse or train ride, the sight of a saloon was like an oasis in the midst of a bleak landscape in winter and a dusty sun-baked horizon during the summer. Few of these places, however, ever matched up to the opulence of Hollywood's 'chandelier palaces' which appear to cover acres. In actual fact Western saloons were quite small, measuring perhaps eighty feet by twenty-four feet. The largest single item was the bar, sometimes twenty or more feet long. There was usually a stove in the centre of the room, windows in the front and occasionally at the back, and a rear door.

The 'facilities' were of the crudest kind and were situated at the rear of the building. Mostly, but not always, they were separated and bore the words 'Gents' or 'Women' on the doors. However, as late as 1879, the residents of Wichita complained to the Mayor and Council about the activities of the frequenters of the Star Saloon and its companion 'Eating Saloon' who were accustomed 'habitually, to urinate' in the backyard. Their petition demanded the immediate removal of the nuisance and for no repetitions of 'a like character'.

Most places tried within their limited space and equipment to provide comfort and a service for their customers. The better ones came up with a wide choice of cigars and liquors, including imported beer – notably Guinness from Ireland.

Apart from sales of liquors, saloons also competed with gambling halls and provided tables and furnished cards and dice for their customers. Around the walls would be reproduction fancy French mirrors and lithographs of some of the world's most famous paintings, many of them nudes. In the early days lighting was by means of kerosine oil lamps, but later some places installed gas, and, later still, electric light.

The Alamo Saloon in Abilene was almost a palace compared with some of its contemporaries. Its proprietors had spared nothing in their efforts to outdo their rivals, and the place was a mecca to most visitors. Writing in 1940 in the Kansas State Historical Society's *Quarterly*, George L. Cushman gave this description of the Alamo:

> It was housed in a long room with a forty-foot frontage on Cedar street, facing west. There was an entrance at either end. At the west entrance were three double glass doors. Inside and along the front of the south side was the bar with its array of carefully polished brass fixtures and rails. From the back bar arose a large mirror, which reflected the brightly sealed bottles of liquor. At various places over the walls were huge paintings in cheaply done imitations of the nude masterpieces of the Venetian Renaissance painters. Covering the entire floor space were gaming tables, at which practically any game of chance

could be indulged. The Alamo boasted an orchestra, which played forenoons, afternoons, and nights. In the height of the season the saloons were the scene of constant activity. At night the noises that were emitted from them were a combination of badly rendered popular music, coarse voices, ribald laughter and Texas 'whoops', punctuated at times by gun shots.

As popular in its way but by no means as opulent, the Gold Room in Newton during 1871 attracted residents and visitors alike. Although one newspaper correspondent noted that the wood was still green and daylight showed through some cracks in the roof and rafters, the place already had a spider population and was also favoured by other insect life. Like most of its contemporaries, the Gold Room did not have the famous batwing doors which are regulation in Western films. This improvement came later. The early saloons were equipped with hinged doors with or without glass panels.

The bar took up a great deal of space as we have noted, and was accompanied by brass foot-rails, the inevitable cuspidor, and surrounded by a liberally strewn carpet of sawdust. Thus the sound of music, the clink of glasses, the shouts of laughter, combined with the smell of stale beer, sweat and tobacco smoke, created an atmosphere that was both congenial and sociable.

The gambling element set the scene for most saloons and the various halls devoted entirely to it. They were a very mixed lot and included some of the most famous characters in the West. Practically all the noted gunfighters were known to take a turn at spinning roulette wheels, tossing dice, or to peer wisely at a hand of cards, the whole time constantly aware of the movements of their opponents in the game, for the least suspicion that anyone was cheating was apt to cause itchy trigger fingers, and the hammer of a Colt pistol would hit a cap and explode forty grains of black powder . . .

71
Luke Short, the dapper little gunfighter, dressed in a manner that would have befitted London Society.

Among the top-notch gunfighters who gambled was Wild Bill Hickok, credited by one contemporary newspaper with being the proprietor of a 'hell' in Junction City in 1867. But most of his gambling was done in somebody else's place. Those that knew him recalled that he would gamble the shirt off his back, and on one occasion enhanced the 'pot' with his last possession, a black and tan terrier. Samuel D. Henry, a boy in Abilene when Hickok was marshal, recalled that he 'had the name of a "square" gambler. When he lost his pile he never drew his gun as did some others, and demanded his money or a part of it back, but took his loss like a "good sport", borrowed another "stake" and "bucked the tiger" again.' Yet he was never a professional in the sense that dapper little Luke Short was. Hickok's gambling was more of a passion.

Luke Short on the other hand (said to be the undertaker's friend because he 'shot em where it didn't show') spent most of his life in saloons and owned a few in his time. It was while operating the famous Dodge City Long Branch saloon in partnership with W. H. Harris in 1883 that Luke fell foul of a local ordinance that nearly led to open war.

The trouble started in 1880 when the State legislature introduced the citizens of the state to the dreaded word that would one day make strong men cry, women mourn and small-time hoodlums into internationally known gangsters – prohibition. At first the amendment to the State Constitution did not have much effect, for the citizens continued to drink and gamble with equanimity, but soon their drinking habits received a jolt. In some places beer and liquor supplies dried up completely, while in others the flow seemed endless. It then became a contest between the 'wet' and 'dry' elements as to who would have the last word.

By 1883 the citizens of Dodge City were about equally divided on the issue and Short was a member of the 'Gang', a semi-political group of gamblers and saloonkeepers who wished the county to remain 'wet' and were opposed by a reform group, led by Alonzo B. Webster and other noted dignitaries who wanted the state to become 'dry'.

Allegations were made that the Gang were responsible for some strong arm tactics and that they rigged games, engaged in stagecoach hold-ups and land frauds, which, combined with Dodge's already 'wicked' reputation, discouraged would-be settlers. Some even claimed that people passing through the region en route to less violent areas were said to end their evening prayers with such remarks as 'and please let us pass through Dodge City safely, Amen'.

Webster was elected mayor of Dodge in 1881 and his administration put a stop to a lot of the alleged criminal activities of the Gang but imposed a number of ordinances designed to restrict the saloon and gambling business. On examination they proved to be thinly disguised efforts to get around the State legislation in order to improve the city's finances, and Luke and his friends were not impressed.

The matter came to head on 28 April 1883, when Luke and his partner deliberately defied an ordinance against prostitution. As a result the police raided the place and arrested his girl 'singer' and charged her with soliciting. Luke was furious. He stormed over to the mayor's office and demanded to know why they had raided him and nobody else. He got no satisfaction there and, as he was returning to his saloon, he met a special policeman named L. C. Hartman, one of the arresting officers. The two started to argue and then swapped lead, but neither was hurt. Other police were soon on hand and Luke found himself in jail. Next, the mayor arrived together with a committee of reformers and Luke was advised to stay out of town permanently, otherwise his health might suffer. Despite his protests, he was put on a train for Topeka where he rushed to the governor and lodged a complaint.

Within days the papers carried stories of Luke's dismissal and the affair was reported as far away as New York. Worse, Luke had sent out an appeal to his friends for help. The news sent a chill of fear around Dodge, for they well knew what it could mean. And they were right. Soon it was learned that Wyatt Earp, Bat Masterson and possibly Doc Holliday (whose presence is not recorded but contemporary accounts indicate that he was on his way) would arrive and sort out Mayor Webster and his cronies. By the end of May the group was well entrenched.

Webster appealed to the governor for help and demanded he send troops. The governor flatly refused but sent a representative along to see just what the problem was. Meanwhile, however, the citizens had seen the error of their ways and Luke was reinstated. To celebrate the event he and his friends posed for a picture which is today familarly known as 'the Dodge City Peace Commission'.

Luke Short's problems with the city fathers were not the

72
The Dodge City Police Commission. Photographed by the Dodge City photographer Conkling, this was the group that finally came to the aid of Luke Short when he and the city's administration fell out. Several versions of this picture are known. In some W. F. Petillon, the champion pie-eater of Dodge, has been substituted for Bill Tilghman, who had little to do with the dispute. This is the original version and the eight men have been identified as follows: back row, left to right; W. H. Harris, Luke Short, Bat Masterson and W. F. Petillon. Front row, left to right; Charles E. Bassett, Wyatt Earp, M. F. McLain (or McLane), and Neil Brown.

last, for barely a year later David 'Mysterious Dave' Mather and his partner named Black opened up the Mather and Black Opera House and Dancehall. Dave was as mysterious as his name implies, and his origin has long been in doubt. But it has now been established by Jack DeMattos that he was born on 10 August 1851 at Saybrook, Connecticut, and christened David Allen Mather. He and his brother Joshua Wright Mather were both residents of Dodge, but it was Dave who commanded most attention.

Old-timer Robert M. Wright recalled that Dave was a wicked man, 'a killer of killers'. If he 'promised a man he would kill him he was sure to do it'. In Dodge, Dave had served briefly on the police force and had fallen out with another famous resident, Thomas Nixon, one of the most noted buffalo hunters of his time. Nixon was on the police force at the time and Dave believed that he was responsible for the Mather and Black Saloon not getting into the dance hall business.

Dave and his partner then started selling their beer at considerably less than the normal price – two glasses for twenty-five cents. Nixon, who was in partnership with a man named Bond, persuaded the other saloonkeepers to put pressure on the wholesalers to cut off Mather's beer supplies. This they did. Mather and Nixon then shot it out, but neither was seriously hurt. Several days later, however, Mather came up

73
'Mysterious Dave' Mather.

behind Nixon and called his name. As he started to turn Mather shot him dead. He went on trial for his life but was acquitted. Most people welcomed the verdict for they believed that Nixon had started the trouble and Mather had been entitled to reprisal – but Bat Masterson always believed that Nixon had not been given the chance for his life that the Western code demanded.

Luke Short, meantime, was still having trouble. Wherever he went it followed him. In 1881 in Tombstone he had shot and killed Charlie Storms, a gunfighter of some reputation, when Storms had deliberately provoked him into a fight. When Short finally left Dodge City following a suit against the city for dismissing him (which was settled out of court), he next appeared as the proprietor of the White Elephant saloon in Fort Worth, Texas, where he quickly became the leading light in the gambling business. Soon complaints were made that Short's organisation was fleecing too many people and the businessmen decided to take action.

The man they chose to put Luke Short out of the way was James Courtright, known to most people as 'Long-haired Jim', whose reputation with a gun rated him high on the list. Down the years all manner of stories have been told and retold about what happened on the night of 8 February 1887, when Short and Courtright came face to face. The most reliable account was given by Short's partner Jake Johnson in court under oath.

Johnson testified that he had talked with Courtright outside the saloon that evening and that he had asked Short to come out. After a brief chat the three men set off down the street and came to a halt outside the Ella Blackwell shooting gallery. Johnson, according to the Fort Worth *Gazette* of 10 February 1887, then declared that 'Courtright and Short were three or four feet apart while talking. Luke had his thumbs in the armholes of his vest [waistcoat], then he dropped them in front of him, when Courtright said, "You needn't be getting out your gun." Luke said, "I haven't got any gun here, Jim," and raised up his vest to show him. Courtright then pulled his pistol. He drew first, and then Short drew his and commenced to fire.'

Another witness standing beside the gallery noted that Courtright hardly got his pistol clear of leather before Short's first shot hit him, and then Short stepped up to him and 'fired four more times after Courtright fell'. It is a part of Texas legend that Courtright had in fact drawn his pistol but Short's first shot blasted his thumb off, and in trying to work the 'border shift' (that is tossing a pistol from one hand to another or both at the same time) he was shot again by Short. The truth was that when they examined Courtright's pistol the cylinder was jammed and would not turn anyway. Short was arrested and released on a $2000 bail but was never convicted.

Not all the noted saloonmen were gunfighters and killers. Some were famous in their own right, many for their ability as pasteboard manipulators or wielders of that instrument of destiny, the dice. One such individual was Richard 'Dick' Clark, perhaps the most impassive and stonefaced of them all. He was born on 15 April 1838, at Cayuga, New York, and christened Richard Brinsley Sheridan Clark after the famous playwright. The family moved to Saginaw, Michigan, and

74
The interior of the Long Branch Saloon, Dodge City, in the 1880s. Here in 1878, Levi Richardson and 'Cock-eyed' Frank Loving shot it out. Eleven shots were fired and no-one but the two participants were hit.

75
The Orient Saloon, Bisbee, Arizona. The scene is a faro layout and the dealer is Harry Emerson, the lookout George Oakes, and the first man on the left is Tony Downs, the part owner. Next to the case keeper is a man described as a 'concert singer named Doyle'. Beyond him is a Bisbee saloonman named Jack Boston and the man in the silk topper is 'Sleepy Tom' Thomas, a well-known gambler.

75

early in life Dick Clark displayed the closemouthed trait of all professional gamblers. He left home before he was twenty and drifted west as far as Denver, where he began to learn in earnest everything there was to know about gambling.

During the Civil War he served in Company H First Colorado Infantry, but once the war was over he was back again in familiar surroundings and free to gamble to his heart's content. He made his way towards the cowtowns and spent some time in Abilene before moving on to the Gold Room in Newton, and later visited Dodge City. Later still he moved to Tombstone. Here he made many friends – far more than he ever did money – and when he died in 1893, the whole of Tombstone mourned his passing.

Unlike Clark, some of the gamblers, whose names meant something at the time, are now lost to history. What kind of men were those with such fascinating names as 'Corn-Hole Johnny', whose real name was John Gallagher? Some called him 'Three-card Johnny', or 'Chuck-luck Johnny'. Then there was Jim Moon, from New York, monte dealers like 'Pony' Reid, and the Texan 'Trick' Brown, all of whom were noted in the early cattle towns. The list is endless. And the saloon set did not stop at the gamblers.

Among the toughest of the saloonkeepers was 'Rowdy Joe' Lowe, a veteran of the Civil War and a noted character in the years immediately following. In company with an equally colourful lady known as 'Rowdy Kate' he set up in business at Ellsworth, Wichita and several parts of Texas. He shot a man named Sweet in Newton for molesting Kate, and in 1873 was the victor in a shoot-out with rival saloonkeeper E. T. 'Red' Beard. Lowe finished off his rival with a shotgun, but the court hearing failed to prove it because of the conflicting evidence. None the less, Lowe decided that he should seek pastures new and he 'partook of leg bail' and disappeared toward Texas one jump ahead of the law – the details of the chase would do justice to any detective yarn. After a very hectic life Joe finally settled in Denver where he was killed in 1899 – ironically unarmed.

Owning or operating a saloon, gambling den or brothel was no pastime for the timid, for those who did were a rough, tough lot and were matched in many respects by the ladies of uneasy virtue who followed the rails and the trails West 'at the service of Mankind'.

76
A gambling scene in a Pecos, Texas, saloon in the 1880s. It is thought that the man in the white hat at the table is Jim Miller, later lynched with three others at Ada, Oklahoma, in 1909.

77
Joseph 'Rowdy Joe' Lowe, Civil War artilleryman, gambler, gunfighter and brothelkeeper. Joe and his equally colourful 'wife', 'Rowdy Kate', livened up every place they settled from Ellsworth and Newton in Kansas to Denison and Fort Worth in Texas.

7 SOILED DOVES AND SISTERS IN SIN

Desperate men and women, in the border towns . . . recognized the law of neither God nor man. But woe to the man who put away a woman against her will.
Samuel D. Henry

Late one night a buffalo hunter left his camp outside Dodge City and meandered into town for a drink and perhaps some feminine company. He strolled toward the beckoning light of a saloon and pushed open the door. Inside the place was crowded and noisy. Suddenly he saw a man at the bar pull his pistol, shove it against the ear of a man standing next to him and blow his brains out. He then calmly carried on drinking his whiskey. At that moment a girl sitting cross-legged on a billiard table jumped down and ran over to the bar. Ignoring the dead man she rubbed her hands in the pool of blood forming on the floor. She then turned and cried out: 'Cock-a doodle-doo!' and clapped her hands together spattering blood all over her dress and those immediately around her. The 'wicked bitch' so upset the buffalo hunter that he felt physically sick and, turning on his heel, went back to his camp and got drunk on his own.

Not all the women of the cattle and mining towns were like that, but most of them were as hard as nails, for without at least a rock hard exterior they could not hope to survive in such places.

Women were by no means rare in the West, but single ones were a much sought-after commodity, and during the raw period when most of the Frontier's population was male, the sight of a respectable woman was an event that might be talked of for weeks. As early as California's gold rush the appearance of women and children in camp caused as much excitement among the love-starved men as did another strike. Some men actually wept at the sight of them.

78
'Squirrel-tooth' Alice was one of the more attractive of Dodge City's 'sisters in sin'. Here she poses with what looks like a live squirrel, complete with lead.

By the late 1860s, however, women were already making their mark and establishing a place in the male-dominated society. The madams and their 'girls' were welcome in any mining camp or cattle town, for apart from their obvious attractions they established a touch of civilisation that most men craved.

Most of the girls lived in small rooms or 'cribs' either attached to, or close by, the saloons or dance halls where they worked. Their rooms were normally placed right at the rear and were set each side of a corridor. The furnishings consisted of a bed, a bowl of water and a jug, a towel and perhaps a mirror. Few of the girls became pregnant because most of them were versed in contemporary methods of birth control. None the less, the various forms of contraception did little to prevent the spread of venereal diseases which, combined with tuberculosis, were the most common complaints in Frontier communities, although the latter was responsible for more deaths among the cowboy population than the former.

So-called 'genteel' sections of society regarded the ladies of uneasy virtue with very mixed feelings, and even the newspapers never missed a chance

79
'Timberline', an early-day Dodge City prostitute. The poor state of the photograph cannot hide the fact that her face is already showing signs of the hard life the women led.

to publicise their activities. According to Don Ashbaugh in his *Nevada's Turbulent Yesterday*, when one of Pioche, Nevada's favourite whores caught pneumonia and died, the whole town mourned her passing, and in true Western tradition they placed the following epitaph on her tombstone:

Here lies the body of Virginia Marlotte,
She was born a virgin and died a harlot.
For eighteen years she preserved her virginity –
That's a damned good record for this vicinity.

Historian Joseph W. Snell in his *Painted Ladies of the Cowtowns*, remarked on the subject of virtue:

> In the very early days of Abilene, Wichita, Ellsworth, Newton, Dodge City and Caldwell, when the summer months brought hundreds of suddenly solvent, whisky-thirsty, woman-hungry cowboys to town if was difficult indeed for virtue to remain intact. Not that the local maidens turned to prostitution in order to increase the family purse – quite the contrary. In those days there was only a very small supply of the domestic variety of females and those were jealously guarded by husbands and fathers.

Hundreds of out-of-state girls and grown women flocked to the cattle centres all anxious to sell their favours for as much as possible, and, provided they could stand the strain, as often as possible.

In some places the activities of the girls were carefully enumerated by those who prepared city directories. A variety of occupations were listed including 'milliner', 'laundress' or 'housekeeper', but occasionally remarks appeared that were less than subtle. Girls were listed with an asterisk which with the passing of time might be meaningless to all but a few with access to contemporary records. Among the remarks could be found such occupations as 'night worker', 'horizontally employed', and 'ceiling expert'. Mr Snell reports that in the Ellsworth census records for 1870 the enumerator used red ink to list the occupation of Libby Thompson who 'diddles', Harriet Parmenter who 'does "horizontal" work', Ettie Baldwin who 'squirms in the dark', and Lizzie Harris who 'Ogles fools'. 'To prevent future generations from mistaking the true character of

80
Tombstone's Bird Cage Theatre was a great attraction. This scantilly-clad 'dove' is 'Heavy Haulin' Mamma'.

these "ladies",' wrote Mr Snell, 'he boldly labelled their residence a "house of ill fame".'

Prostitution was not of course limited to the Kansas cowtowns, for the oldest profession was widely practised in all the mining camps and railroad end-of-track sites where tents were erected which would be taken down and put up at the next halt. Better pickings were to be made in some of the Eastern cities, but perhaps because the West attracted such a mixture of humanity, and the opportunity to get rich quick, its uncivilised atmosphere always attracted more girls than elsewhere.

Newton, according to a correspondent for the Wichita *Tribune* on 24 August 1871, had barely become populated before it had ten bawdy houses 'in full running order and three more under way'. The places were overflowing with rotten whiskey, rogues, gamblers and lewd men and women who seemed

81
And there were respectable gals, like Nellie Cashman, an early-day Tombstoneite, whose favours and virtues earned her the title of 'the Angel of the Camp'. She befriended many a down-and-outer.

to run the town. He claimed to have been in many such places, 'but Newton is the fastest one I have ever seen. Here you may see young girls not over sixteen drinking whisky, smoking cigars, cursing and swearing until one almost loses the respect they should have for the weaker sex. I heard one of their townsmen say he didn't believe there were a dozen virtuous women in town. This speaks well for a town claiming 1500 inhabitants . . .'

Social limitations aside, the girls were a good source of revenue for the town councils. Available records show that fines for prostitution or for keeping a brothel or bawdy house varied from town to town. Miller and Snell report that Wichita fined ladies $8 per month plus $2 court costs. But brothelkeepers were fined $18 per month plus $2 court costs. For selling whiskey they were required to pay a flat licence fee of $25 per month. Other places had similar rates, and it depended on the city council (or the zealousness of the police) how often the girls were arrested and fined. But as certain members of police forces were known to frequent brothels, action was sometimes unforthcoming.

State laws labelled prostitution and brothelkeeping as a misdemeanor punishable by fines of up to $1000 and the possibility of a county jail sentence of as much as six months. Understandably, had those rules been followed the state and not the local administration would have benefited, so subtle changes were made. Local fines were imposed and collected on a monthly basis. Gamblers and liquor sellers also came within this ruling and sometimes it led to dispute. 'Rowdy Joe' Lowe and 'Rowdy Kate' were notorious tax evaders and were frequently in trouble with the law. But the fines achieved their object – the

82
Lotta Crabtree, a Siren of the 1880s and the Belle of the Bird Cage.

city coffers grew rich on the proceeds.

One obvious use to which some of these monies was put was in providing payment for a sometimes expensive police force. Occasionally such expense caused a serious drain on city finances. This happened in Dodge City in 1878 when Bat Masterson's brother Edward J. Masterson was killed in a street fight (details can be found in Chapter 8) and deputy US marshal Harry T. McCarty was shot dead by a lunatic as he sat in the Long Branch Saloon. The Dodge City authorities then hired four policemen, which badly affected the city's finances. Stringent measures were called for and, according to Mr Snell, on 6

83
Suffolk-born 'Poker Alice' Tubbs (1851-1930), a noted gambler, whose motto was: 'I never run a crooked game and never gamble on a Sunday.' One weekday she shot a drunken soldier dead. Said the judge: 'I cannot find it in my heart to send a white-haired old lady to prison,' and let her go free.

August three revenue-producing ordinances were passed. One of them dealt specifically with brothels and stated that 'any person whether male or female being an inmate or resident of any brothel, bawdy house or house of ill-fame in this city shall upon conviction thereof be fined in a sum not less than Five or more than Fifty Dollars.' A brothelkeeper was liable to fines of from $5 to $100. The other ordinances were equally as harsh. There were fines of from $10 to $100 for gambling, and a tax on all real, personal and mixed property.

The antics of the cyprian sisters never failed to delight the readers of Frontier newspapers. The Ford County *Globe* on 21 January 1879 noted a fight between two 'fascinating doves of the roost' (in this instance a boarding house on Tin Pot Alley):

> When we heard the noise and looked out the front window, which commanded a view of the situation, it was a magnificent sight to see. Tufts of hair, calico, snuff and gravel flew like fur in a cat fight, and before we could distinguish how the battle waned a chunck of dislocated leg grazed our ear and a cheer from the small boys announced that a battle was lost and won. The crowd separated as the vanquished virgin was carried to her parlors by two 'soups'. A disjointed nose, two or three internal bruises, a chawed ear and a missing eye were the only scars we could see.

Sometimes the women fought for fun, and sometimes men and women fought each other. According to the Topeka *Commonwealth* of 20 September 1871, Bill Dow and Lottie Foster had a showdown in Newton. Dow was a well known character (in Wichita he was known as 'Rattlesnake Bill'), and Miss Foster was a former 'demi-rep' from Topeka. Several days before, Dow had beaten her 'badly and put a cap on one of her peepers. Lottie, disliking the manliness which characterized her interview with Dow, acquired a revolver and as he was passing along the street, fired five shots, the fifth taking effect in his hip, inflicting a very severe wound. Dow still lives and will probably survive the deadly assault.' It was later reported that Lottie had 'abandoned her wicked life' and had gone to the Cincinnatti Home for Friendless Women.

A less serious assault occurred in Dodge City in 1877, when a man struck 'a woman in labour' – in her case she was ironing. Noted the *Times:*

> The office of City Attorney [Harry E. Gryden] was thrown into extatic convulsions at precisely 4:30 P.M., Monday, by the appearance of Fannie. (Fannie is a beauty, and the color of a Colorado Claro, as found at Beatty & Kelly's.) She complained of one James Cowan (Maduro color) and on the case being tried Mr. Gryden developed the following facts: that Fanny was peacefully ironing at the residence of Mrs. Curly, when James entered (three-sheets-in-the-wind drunk) called Fannie a soldier b———, throwed her on the floor, elevated her paraphanalia, spanked her, and finally busted her a left hander in the right eye, accompanying the same with a kick in the stomach. The City Attorney went to the court and for the defendant, touched up the Louisiana and South Carolina questions, and closed by flinging the star spangled banner over the contraband female, sending the defendant to the regions of the unjust – $5 and costs.

Some famous gunfighters had their moments of confrontation with angry 'doves'. One particularly famous incident concerned Miss Frankie Bell, a well known Dodge City whore whose 'vocation was intoxication', especially during the festive season. However, when she met Wyatt Earp in July 1877, she let him know what she thought of him in no uncertain manner. On 21 July the *Times* noted that Mr Earp was very annoyed and promptly slapped her, which caused an uproar. She ended up in the 'dog house' as the city jail was affectionately known, and the next morning had a 'reception at the police court . . . the expense of which was about $20.00.' Wyatt Earp was also fined – the lowest limit of the law, $1!

But what were they like these now legendary women? For every one that got her name into a newspaper, court record or a coroner's report, there were a hundred that simply disappeared into obscurity. Some we know married their clients and their descendants are not anxious for publicity. But what of the rest?

The women came from almost anywhere; practically every European nationality was

84 and 85

Martha Jane Cannary – 'Calamity Jane' – was born around 1844, 1850 or 1852, depending on which version you accept, and most of her life is as obscure, not least because even by Western standards, she was a notable liar. That she and Wild Bill Hickok were lovers is sheer myth, but she seems to have been a warm-hearted gal. She died in 1903. Her attachment to male attire suggested to one historian that she may have suffered from some form of 'pseudo-hermaphroditism'. This was refuted by one old-timer who declared: 'I don't care what religion she was – I like to read about her!'

represented and, occasionally, the Far East. They appeared in all sizes and shapes. Some were very pretty; but whether they were or not did not really matter. Some were downright mean, carried knives or pistols in the most unlikely places – and would use them too if clients got out of hand or insisted on 'variations' which they would not accept. Yet all realised that they were at a premium and were determined to make what they could while they could. Age, too, was no barrier. Mr Snell has observed that there were some women as old as forty, but those over thirty were the exceptions rather than the rule, for most of the girls were in their 'teens or early twenties. However, he did note that at least one girl was fourteen. He concluded that many of them married or simply gave it up.

Some women entered the profession unwittingly, fully convinced that the advertisements for domestics and other apparently harmless occupations were bona fide. Only when they arrived – with a one way ticket – did they realise their terrible error. A lucky few escaped; but for the others there was none, and it was women such as these who found that the constant degradation, abuse, threat of disease and depravity had only one end – death. Some died naturally, but far more took their own lives. A common method was some form of poison, laudanum being the most readily available.

But sometimes a girl killed herself for the most human reason of all – she fell in love with a customer. This happened to a girl in Newton in September 1871. She loved a railroad man but he was not interested. Distraught she first tried poison, but could not get the right stuff, so she next acquired a pistol.

Once inside her room she cocked it, jammed the muzzle against her stomach and pulled the trigger . . .

Moments later the place was crowded, but there was nothing they could do. They made her comfortable and at her request sent for the man she loved. He came, reluctantly, and doubtless squirmed, for, as the Kansas City *Times* described it: 'her eyes never left him from the moment he entered until the film of death shut out all sight of the outer world . . .'

Occasionally women turned to prostitution because they were deserted by their husbands, and with families to support, there was no other way to make money. It is claimed that Wyatt Earp deserted his second wife, Mattie Baylock, in Tombstone (although no actual records have been uncovered to prove their marriage). Wyatt went off with a saloon girl named Josephine Sarah Marcus. Mattie turned to prostitution and finally took an overdose of laudanum and died. Wyatt may or may not have known of her tragic end, for he and Sarah were long gone; but perhaps he lived to regret his association with Sarah, because she 'gave him hell' in his final years.

86
Belle Starr was a flamboyant female outlaw. She was killed by an unknown assassin in 1889.

The death of a prostitute in most cowtowns and mining camps affected her customers but not many others. Occasionally, however, as with Virginia Marlotte, there were those who mourned her. Another such a woman was Dora Hand, of local reputation during her lifetime, but now a part of Western legend.

Dora Hand's real name was Fannie Keenan and she appeared in Dodge City in 1878 where she was employed as a 'singer', but she soon established friendships with some of the most prominent men in town. Among these was the mayor, James 'Dog' Kelley. On the night of 4 October she was asleep in a room belonging to Mayor Kelley who was in Fort Dodge being treated for an illness. As she slept, a man named James Kenedy, son of a wealthy Texas cattleman, crept up to the wall of the room and fired four shots through it. He then ran to his horse, mounted it and made his escape. He had a grudge against the mayor and had decided to kill him. Only when a posse led by Bat Masterson and Wyatt Earp had caught up with him and wounded him in his left shoulder did he learn of his terrible error. Dora Hand was dead and Kenedy was in danger of being lynched.

Back in Dodge the wounded man was placed under guard and when he was well enough, he was examined before Judge R. G. Cook. But for reasons which are still not clear, he was acquitted. His father came up from Texas to take him home, but not before his son had undergone very painful surgery to remove bits of shattered bone from his shoulder. Dora was given a magnificent funeral and practically every citizen of Dodge was present.

These then were the women, good, bad, pretty and ugly, over whom men fought and died for their favours. Without them the West would have been a much less colourful place.

8 TAMING THE COWTOWNS

When you heard one or two shots, you waited breathlessly for a third. A third shot meant a death on Texas Street.
Stuart Henry

With a whoop, a rush and a roar, a crowd of Texas cowboys raced their ponies down to the creek, splashed their way across and, once more on firm ground, spurred them on to a mad gallop. Seconds later they were on the main street, their wild cries punctuated by pistol shots. All around them people ran for cover afraid that they would be the next target. All except for one man.

He stood coatless, his white shirt stark in the glare of the sunlight. Around his hips hung twin cartridge belts, and from low-slung holsters the butts of two Colt pistols were readily to hand. Pinned to his shirt front was a gleaming star. Calmly he waited for the riders to reach him, and as they pounded up he raised his left arm.

'Hold it, boys,' he ordered. 'That's far enough.'

Obediently the Texans hauled down on the reins and brought their struggling mounts to a slithering halt, and as the dust settled they looked down sheepishly at the big man in front of them.

'Sorry, boys,' he said, 'but the rules are no guns in town – you can leave 'em at my office and pick 'em up on the way out.'

For a long moment they were silent, then they shrugged their shoulders, holstered their pistols and walked their horses over to his office. One turned in the saddle and grinned: 'You win, Marshal, we don't want no trouble!'

That scene could have come from any of a hundred Western films or books, and is typical of the legend that has grown around the two-gun marshals, the town-tamers who policed the Western cowtowns, mining camps and railroad end-of-track cities. These were the men whose iron nerve, incorruptibility, and skill with firearms had made their particular towns safe to live in, to bring up children and to build schools and hospitals and give the place a future. Such is the idealised portrait of the town-tamer, and there were certainly some men of that ilk whose devotion to duty and self-sacrifice give credit to the legend, but the 'lone man against evil' . . . well, it was never quite like that.

The more populated the West became, the more determined were people to bring in law and order as quickly as possible. Depending on its population and location, a town was granted a status of first, second or third-class city, and on that basis it was governed. Once authority was received to act, the responsible citizens organised a police force, and the other officials necessary to administer the place. Fortunately, some Kansas towns were well organised by the time they joined the cattle trade, but others were not. Such a place was Abilene.

During the first cattle shipping season of late 1867 there had been little trouble. None the less, the citizens realised that as each season arrived the numbers of cattle and men would increase and it was only a matter of time before violence broke out. The only law in Dickinson County (in which Abilene is situated) was a constable in Grant Township which was not enough, and by the middle of 1869 the Texans had all but taken over the town. The citizens reacted against their violence and several battles took place between them and the cowboys. In retaliation some of the Texans set fire to property and took pot shots at people as they galloped past.

A hastily constructed jail was destroyed, so an armed guard made sure the next one was erected without incident. But the violence continued. Men even rode their horses into saloons and terrified women on the streets. Once the pistols began to go off day and night the honest citizens found it wisest to be within reach of shelter.

It was an intolerable situation, and in September 1869, the citizens persuaded the probate judge of Dickinson County to grant them the status of a third-class city which meant that they could hold elections. A board of trustees was then set up and this body remained in control until April 1871. As the cattle season of 1870 approached one very important decision was made – to create the position of, and appoint, a marshal. An ordinance was passed banning the carrying of firearms and running gambling establishments and brothels within city limits. The problem was to enforce it, although the alleged thirty-two saloons of the previous season were now down to about ten, and the town also boasted of five general stores and four hotels.

The position of marshal was created on 2 May, but it was 4 June before the job was filled successfully. On that date the man who was to leave his mark on the town was hired at $150 a month. He was Thomas James Smith.

Smith's early life remains obscure. According to the 1870 Census he was forty years old and had been born in New York which could have meant the state rather than the city. In 1904 T. C. Henry, the chairman of the board of trustees who had acted as mayor until 1871, alleged that Abilene's Tom Smith was the same man who had led a riot of railroad workers at Bear River, or Bear Town, Wyoming Territory, in November 1868, while employed as trouble-shooter for the Union Pacific Railway. But what Henry and the others did not know was that for his part in it, the Tom Smith who led the riot

87
Tom Smith, Marshal of Abilene in 1870, who tamed the town by a combination of fearless personality and sledgehammer fists, much to the discomforture of the Texans. Murdered after the cattle season was over, he 'died a martyr to duty', as his monument, erected in 1904, recalls, 'a fearless hero of frontier days, who in cowboy chaos established the supremacy of law.'

had been sent to the State Penitentiary, and despite some intensive research into official records, it is still not known if they were one and the same man – if not, then Abilene's Tom Smith would certainly not appreciate his now legendary 'Bear River Tom' tag.

Also in the legendary category is the story that Tom Smith was once a New York policeman, that he did something, or something happened to him, to make him go West. It may be true. His manner was that of a good cop. Smith proved himself a very worthy peace officer and during his period in office dramatic changes came about. Firearms were placed out of bounds (although they did not entirely disappear as some writers have claimed) and slowly but surely the big man on the silver-grey horse, named 'Silverheels', who rode slowly up and down Texas Street several times a day, gained not only the trust of the citizens but their respect and admiration as a policeman. His deputy was a young Canadian, James H. McDonald.

Henry's 1904 recollections included a number of anecdotes about Smith that may well be true, although they escaped contemporary records. He claimed that 'Big Hank', a cowboy desperado, was the first man to challenge Smith's reign when he refused to give up his gun. Smith promptly slammed one of his big fists into the cowboy's face and when he came round ordered him to leave town. The cowboys were amazed. No one had tried anything like that before – as far as they were concerned a man fought with a knife or a gun, not his fists; and Smith's were in the sledgehammer class.

'Wyoming Frank', another would-be marshal deflater, made his attempt one Sunday, but was baffled when Smith refused to pull his gun. Swearing horribly he allowed himself to be taken back into a saloon, and then he exploded into violence, but before his gun cleared leather Smith had hit him and he went down. 'I'll give you five minutes to get out of this town, and don't you ever come back,' growled Tom Smith, and the Texan took him at his word.

That Smith could use the two silver-mounted Colt pistols he wore in his belt no one doubted, but his methods baffled most of the Texans so much that they avoided him.

By 9 August his salary had risen from $150 a month to the amazing sum of $225 – the highest known figure ever paid to an old-time cowtown marshal. He also served as a deputy and under-sheriff of the county, and some sources claim he was appointed a deputy US marshal.

During the summer of 1870 Abilene relished its first real taste of law and order. Although the cattle business was booming and more and more cowboys were appearing in town, few felt brave enough to tackle Tom Smith and Jim McDonald. But within weeks of the cattle season ending, there was tragedy. At the request of the county sheriff, Joseph Cramer, who was a dying man, Smith and McDonald went out to Chapman Creek to arrest a man named Andrew McConnell charged with the murder of a settler named John Shea. McConnell, aided by his neighbour, Moses Miles, resisted arrest and in the struggle Smith was shot by McConnell and all but decapitated by Miles who attacked his body with an axe. McDonald exchanged shots with both men and shot off two of Miles's fingers before both men escaped, and McDonald returned to Abilene for assistance.

A furious posse set out in pursuit and the two men were captured near Clay Centre. Fears of lynching kept them on the move from one county to another until they finally went on trial in March 1871, where each man received a prison sentence instead of death – much to the disgust of Abilene's citizens who made no bones about it: 'Them varmints should've stretched rope!' growled one old-timer bitterly, summing up the feelings of all.

88
A rare tintype of Wild Bill Hickok made around 1863-4, some seven years before he became Tom Smith's successor at Abilene in 1871. This is how he looked when he was a contract scout and spy for the Union Army in the Civil War, a dangerous job that would have resulted in a firing squad if caught. Records prove he was 'a good man for the Union'.

But Tom Smith's death posed a problem. Who would succeed him? As a stopgap, gunsmith Patrick Hand was made marshal, but he was replaced later by McDonald who is listed as a policeman. Apparently, his heroic attempt to stop the murderers of Smith had not been appreciated by many of the locals, and it was openly stated that he had 'turned and run', which doubtless upset McDonald very much.

On 3 April 1871, the first municipal elections were held in the city and Joseph G. McCoy, the 'father of the cattle trade' was elected mayor. His first task, he recalled many years later, was to find a marshal. His book-keeper, Charles Gross, suggested a man he had known some years earlier back in Illinois, and who even now was reputed to be the most feared gunfighter in the West – James Butler Hickok, then known by no other name but 'Wild Bill'.

During the eight months that he was Marshal of Abilene, Wild Bill showed a completely different approach to the job than had Tom Smith. Smith, the mystery man, whose silver-plated Colt pistols were always in evidence but seldom drawn, was the complete opposite to Wild Bill, whose reputation as a gunfighter and marksman was second to none. Few men cared to provoke Hickok into dropping his hands to the ivory butts of the twin Colt Navy pistols he wore stuck in his belt, butts forward.

It was the threat of those pistols and his willingness to use them if the need arose that kept Abilene fairly quiet during the summer of 1871, its greatest and last season as a cattle shipping centre. Just as the season ended Hickok was involved in the one gunfight that marred the comparative peacefulness of his reign and we shall see what happened in the next chapter.

Abilene's citizens had tried hard during that season of 1871 to find a means of cutting down the brothels and gambling hells that existed on Texas Street. They had even moved the whole lot to a fresh site a quarter of a mile away, but there were still problems, for more and more gamblers and prostitutes were being attracted to the place. Hickok and his deputies had their work cut out to keep the peace. Finally the town had had enough, and the order went out to the marshal: 'Close down the brothels and gambling dens!' Within days the trains going east and west were crowded with what the editor of the Abilene *Chronicle* described as:

> . . . vast numbers of sinful humanity. Prostitutes, 'pimps', 'gamblers', 'cappers', [gamblers' decoys] and others of like ilk, finding their several nefarious avocations no longer remunerative or appreciated in their neighbourhood, are embracing their earliest possible convenience, by hook (mostly by *hook*) and by crook, to obtain the necessary wherewithal with which to procure passage to Newton, Kansas City, or St. Louis where in all probability most of them will end their miserable lives in dens of shame – unless the better angel in their nature leads them to forsake the paths of sin.

The end of the cattle season and a determination by the citizens that never again would they 'submit to the evils of the cattle trade' led to the despatch of a long notice to the Texans requesting that they take their cattle elsewhere in the coming season. Hickok was now an expensive liability, so on 13 December 1871, the town council of Abilene dismissed him. But many of them agreed with the editor of the *Chronicle* who had remarked of him: 'We think he is entitled to the thanks of law-abiding citizens throughout the State for the safety of life and property at Abilene, which has been secured, more through his daring, than any other agency.'

Even before Abilene's demise as a cowtown, others had been taking more than a passing interest in the trade. The most important at this time was Newton, in Harvey County, and about thirty miles from Wichita. The Santa Fe Railway reached the town on 17 July 1871, and by August there were a number of saloons and about ten dance halls, many of which also incorporated a brothel. Soon, however, the town's growth was such that twenty-seven saloons and a variety of gambling hells added to the entertainment. The prostitutes and others flocked to the place and occupied a district known locally as 'Hide Park'. An additional attraction at the saloons, gambling dens and presumably the brothels, was a 'free lunch'. But most important of all there was no law.

The fate of the town depended on a ballot which took place on 11 August when the citizens voted on a proposal to issue $20,000 in county bonds to help build the Wichita and Southwestern Railroad. The citizens approved the scheme but during the period of the election a number of special policemen hired to control the crowds were themselves in trouble. Two of them, a Texan named Bill Wilson, sometimes known as Bill Bailey, and an Ohioan named Mike McCluskie (alias Art Delaney) had reputations as bad men. The pair quarrelled and in a gunfight Wilson was killed. McCluskie, already unpopular with the Texans, was advised to leave town 'for his health' until things quietened down. He did, but soon returned and was involved in one of the West's most sensational gunfights – 'The Newton General Massacre' which is featured in the next chapter.

Following the massacre the citizens took action against the lawless element and on 25 August an election was held and two policemen were appointed, Carlos B. King and Thomas Carson, an erstwhile policeman in Abilene. King was killed soon afterward by a drunken ruffian who shot him in the chest with a derringer and escaped. Carson, who was as unpopular in Newton as he had been in Abilene, left soon afterwards and returned to join Hickok's force, but was shortly dismissed for shooting a bartender in the hip without provocation. He was so unpredictable that Hickok advised him to seek pastures new, but he was still around Abilene in January 1872 when he and Brocky Jack Norton (another of Hickok's deputies) shot it out. He was arrested and jailed for wounding Norton (who recovered). Shortly afterwards Carson and three others escaped from jail and were not recaptured – perhaps the authorities thought they were well rid of them.

Another of Hickok's deputies, James H. McDonald, who had been fired from the Abilene police force on 2 September 1871, then became Marshal of Newton, and by all accounts did a good job. In the October he chased a man to Humboldt, Kansas, who had stolen $400 and a fine gold watch, and in the process of arresting him, also arrested another man wanted on a horse-stealing charge. 'McDonald', noted the Oxford, Kansas, *Times*, 'appears to be a wide awake, efficient marshal'. But by November McDonald had left Newton and gone on to Kansas City. The press carried a report that Hickok had been offered the job as marshal of Newton at $200 a month, but he did not take it. Instead the town drifted through the winter of 1871-2 without law until the appointment of William L. Brooks early in April.

Billy Brooks, an erstwhile stagecoach driver, buffalo hunter and Frontier tough, enjoyed a reputation as a bad man and was soon in trouble. He got into a shooting scrape with some Texans in a dance hall and was wounded but managed to give chase to his assailants.

Two other places, Wichita and Ellsworth, vied with Abilene and Newton for the cattle trade in the early 1870s, and each enjoyed a lurid reputation for violence. Ellsworth had been established in 1867, so was a thriving community by the time it took on the formidable task of becoming the main shipping point for Texas cattle. A steady trickle of beef had made its way to the town since its founding, but not until July 1871 did the figures achieve noticeable proportions when an estimated 35,000 head had been shipped east from its rapidly growing stockyards.

Ellsworth had endured a number of brawls and shootouts since its beginning, but the citizens had learned very early on that it paid to have law and order, especially when every other building in town was reputed to be a saloon. The county was also named Ellsworth and in August 1867, it held its first election. Hickok was an unsuccessful candidate for town marshal as he was also in the November elections for county sheriff. Although he polled more votes than anybody else within city limits he did not receive much support from the citizens living in the outlying areas.

By late 1869 the cattle business in Ellsworth was steadily increasing. The law was ready and waiting for the Texans, although in May of that year there was one serious incident that marred a fairly peaceful coexistence between the townspeople and the lawless element. On the 12th a man was dragged from jail where he was awaiting trial for murder, and lynched. Several prominent citizens were even shot at but there were no more incidents.

Ellsworth's brief period as a cowtown is remembered chiefly for the colourful characters who either helped control it or populate the local 'Boot Hill'.

In August 1869, the police force included a well known 'good bad man' named William 'Apache Bill' Semans, an ex-army scout who had the distinction of being of the few who had lost himself and the soldiers he was supposed to be guiding.

'Apache Bill' was a character. Early in May 1869, he had been arrested by a deputy US marshal and charged with 'misappropriating Government property' which in his case was horses and mules belonging to the United States Army. Bill denied his guilt and the Topeka press, who were feuding with some of the US marshals' deputies, and felt an active dislike of the district judge, pointed out that 'Apache Bill' had been arrested four times on alleged horse-stealing charges and each time there had been no evidence. The jury found Bill not guilty and he was discharged, but there is some evidence that Hickok, himself also a deputy US marshal, was in Topeka at the time and

JAMES BUTLER 'WILD BILL' HICKOK

By the time he became Marshal of Abilene in 1871, Wild Bill Hickok was a living legend. In appearance he stood over six feet tall, with shoulder-length auburn hair, a blonde or straw-coloured moustache, and piercing blue-grey eyes that 'stared one right through'. In dress he resembled the Mississippi gamblers and delighted in Prince Albert frock coats, embroidered silk waistcoats, and 'salt and pepper' trousers tucked into knee-high boots or pulled down over them. Around his waist he wore a silk sash into which he thrust an ornately engraved pair of ivory-butted Colt .36 calibre Navy revolvers, worn butts forward for a cross or underhand draw.

He was born at Homer, Illinois (later renamed Troy Grove), on 27 May 1837. In 1856 he left home for Kansas to buy farming land for the family, but was soon embroiled in the Kansas-Missouri Border wars. After a short period as a constable at Montecello Township, he became a stagecoach driver and later, during the Civil War, was employed by the Union army first as a wagonmaster and then as a scout, courier and spy.

Following the war he was active in the Indian wars of the 1860s as an army scout in Kansas and Colorado. He also served a two year period as a deputy US marshal. At Hays City, Kansas, in August 1869, he was elected acting sheriff of Ellis County to fill a vacancy until the regular November election. While in office he killed two men when attempting to maintain law and order. He lost the November election to his deputy and went to Topeka. He returned to Hays in July 1870 to visit friends and was attacked by a number of drunken Seventh Cavalry troopers in Paddy Welche's saloon. Hickok shot two of them, one of whom died, and he was forced to flee the wrath of their friends.

After leaving Abilene he visited friends in various parts of the West and in August 1873 was reluctantly persuaded by his friend Buffalo Bill Cody to join his Combination, a theatrical group performing Wild West plays on the stages of eastern theatres. By March 1874, Hickok had had enough and he returned West. In March 1876, he married Agnes Lake Thatcher whom he had first met in Abilene when she appeared with her circus in 1871. Leaving Agnes with relatives he left for Deadwood with his friend Colorado Charlie Utter to join the goldseekers. His reputation preceded him and many believed that he would be asked to bring law and order to the then lawless and illegal town (built on what was still an Indian Reservation). He was murdered by Jack McCall, a hired assassin, who shot him through the back of the head as he sat playing cards in Saloon No 10 on the afternoon of 2 August 1876. McCall was acquitted by a miners' jury (some claimed they were bribed), but was arrested some weeks later and tried legally, found guilty and hanged on 1 March 1877.

His contemporaries viewed Wild Bill Hickok with mixed feelings, but among the men who actually knew him he was regarded as a man of great courage and integrity, as a firm friend and probably one of the finest pistol shots on the frontier. None of them had even heard of what we today call the 'fast draw' but all credited him with an athletic agility combined with a reflex action that was 'truly remarkable'. With his passing many felt that something of the Old West had also died.

spoke up for him. Unfortunately for 'Apache Bill' his freedom was short-lived. During a disturbance in an Ellsworth dance hall, policeman Semans was shot dead by a Texan whom he tried to stop disturbing the peace.

The cattle continued to flow into the town in ever increasing numbers and with them came more pimps, prostitutes and innumerable gamblers. Joseph G. McCoy also appeared and brought with him from Abilene part of his famous Drover's Cottage, a three storey hotel-cum-meeting place that he had had built in 1867. This was set up in town and rivalled the Grand Central Hotel as a 'desirable residence'.

Refugees from Abilene also included Brocky Jack Norton who, having recovered from his wound at the hand of Tom Carson, applied to join the police force. Chauncey Whitney who was now county sheriff resigned as city marshal and his place was taken by John L. Councell. Norton became his assistant. Both were fired in July and replaced by Edward O. Hogue, who assumed the title 'Chief of Police', but later this was changed to city marshal.

Edward Hogue was fired from his position of marshal on 8 October 1872, and replaced by Brocky Jack Norton, but he remained on the force as a policeman. In this capacity he arrested Ben Thompson's brother Billy on 11 June 1873, for disturbing the peace. Thompson fired his pistol in the street and Hogue was quickly on the scene. Billy was fined $5 and $10 costs. His actions did not please his brother Ben who had arrived in Ellsworth to set up in the saloon business and was not anxious for publicity. However, Ben changed his mind about saloonkeeping and decided that gambling was more profitable.

That summer of 1873 was a bad one for the cattle trade, and this combined with the heat of the season soon had tempers frayed. A feud sprang up between the police force and the Texans, whose anger was directed at one man in particular – John 'Happy Jack' Morco, an illiterate, surly character who had, it was said, killed twelve

89
Ben Thompson, dressed like a true 'City Gent', complete with cane. Born in Yorkshire in 1842, he reached Texas in 1849, serving in the Second Texas Cavalry in the Civil War, then with the Emperor Maximilian in Mexico. After the Emperor's death in 1867, Ben became a gambler in Texas, then Kansas. Finally, with his friend John 'King' Fisher, he was murdered in San Antonio in 1884.

men in gunfights. His appearance on the police force in June was a surprise, for only a week before he had been arrested for vagrancy.

Morco's moody and unpredictable nature made him a man to avoid. He delighted in arresting Texans and on 30 June he arrested Billy Thompson on a charge of assault with a pistol. Billy paid a fine of $10 and $15 costs which coming so soon after his arrest by Hogue aroused bad feelings among the Texans. Ellsworth simmered in the summer heat and everyone expected trouble.

The big event in the Ellsworth violence stakes occurred on 15 August when Ben Thompson fell out with gambler John Sterling over a monte game. Ben had staked him on the understanding that if he won anything Ben would get half. Sterling won $1000 but made himself scarce when Ben heard about it. Ben finally cornered him in Nick Lentz's saloon, and asked him for his money. Sterling promptly slapped Ben in the face, but before Ben could retaliate Morco jumped between them, pulled his pistol and made Ben leave.

90
Chauncey B. Whitney, ex-soldier, scout and, finally, sheriff, who was killed by a drunken Billy Thompson – Ben's brother – one hot August day in 1873.

Ben went straight to Brennan's saloon, and was told that both Morco and Sterling were waiting for him and that they were armed. Ben wasted no time, ducked out of the back door and ran to Jack New's saloon where he had left his Winchester rifle and a pistol. At that moment Billy came in carrying Ben's fine handsome English shotgun (made by George Gibbs of Bristol), and together the brothers stepped on to the street.

Billy, who was drunk, staggered and discharged one of the shotgun barrels. The hail of buckshot narrowly missed the feet of two Texans who hastily got off the street. The brothers then walked towards the railroad. Here they believed they could fight without injuring innocent bystanders.

Sheriff Chauncey Whitney, hearing of the disturbance, ran from his home to try and talk the brothers into surrendering, but already Ben had issued his challenge to Morco and Sterling: 'Bring out your men if you want to fight!' None the less, Whitney persuaded the Thompsons to come back with him to Brennan's saloon. Somebody shouted that Morco was coming for him with a gun, and Ben dashed outside and fired at him. The ball smacked into the door jamb of a store, but Morco swiftly dodged inside the building before Ben could fire again. Billy then came running out of the saloon closely followed by Whitney. Suddenly, Billy turned and pointed the shotgun at the sheriff who

BOOT HILL

'Boot Hill', the traditional burial ground for bad men and others who have died with their boots on, is now an essential part of the Western myth.

The original Boot Hill was at Hays City and it was started on almost the same day that the city was established in 1867. Helping to populate it were the railroad workers, buffalo hunters and soldiers from nearby Fort Hays – although army victims were normally buried at the post. Two of Wild Bill Hickok's victims were buried there – Bill Mulrey or Mulvy, and Samuel Strawhun – and others, good and bad, during the hectic 1860s and early 1870s.

In 1918, twenty-five bodies were discovered on the site of the old Boot Hill and were placed in one container and reburied in the Mount Allen Cemetery with a marker explaining their origin. Later, in April 1947, workmen excavating for new homes discovered eight more bodies, and press reports at the time stated that the workmen expected to uncover the remains of another eight or twelve. Today there are no plans to disturb the ground, but perhaps some future developer may discover yet more victims in that quiet, sinister hill north of town.

Abilene is credited with a Boot Hill as were other places, but the most famous was at Dodge City. In 1878 the *Times* noted that 'Dodge boasts two burying spots, one for the tainted, whose very souls were steeped by immorality, and who have generally died with their boots on. 'Boot-Hill' is the somewhat singular title applied to the burial place of the class just mentioned. The other is not designated by any particular title, but is supposed to contain the bodies of those who died with a clean sheet on their bed – the soul in this case is a secondary consideration.'

By the middle years of this century Dodge's Boot Hill was long gone, but thanks to the continuing publicity the town was receiving, it was decided to reinstate it, and to create the right 'atmosphere' a number of 'concrete boots' were dotted around to suggest hasty burial. To add to the illusion a 'genuine hanging tree from Wyoming' was imported and set up at its edge. Needless to say, criticism by hecklers was not appreciated, especially when one of them pointed out that the tree was on castors. 'Tell me,' he asked, 'do you hire it out for lynchings?'

hastily backed away. 'Don't shoot,' he pleaded, but Billy callously jerked the trigger and the boom of the shotgun and Whitney's screams of agony brought crowds of men to the street.

Ben was beside himself with grief and rage at what his brother had done, but he still found time to urge him to leave town, and fast. 'You've shot Whitney, our best friend!' he shouted at him. Billy shook his head and stared at his brother through an alcoholic haze and shrugged his shoulders. 'I don't give a damn, and would have shot him even if he had been Jesus Christ,' he mumbled. But Ben grabbed him and pushed him toward a horse, and moments later, swaying in the saddle, Billy trotted out of town leaving Ben to face the now furious townsfolk.

For an hour Ben held the town at bay before surrendering to Hogue on the understanding that Morco was also disarmed. The police force were all fired and Hogue was reappointed marshal. Whitney, who, despite his terrible wound, claimed that Billy had shot him by accident, lingered for three days and died in great agony on the 18th. It was 1877 before Billy was arrested and placed on trial in Ellsworth for the killing, but he was acquitted, some believed because the jury had been bribed.

The most important by-product of the Whitney shooting was the claim made by his biographer, Stuart Lake, that Wyatt Earp had stepped out of the crowd and heroically arrested Ben Thompson when no one else would dare. Unfortunately for Mr Earp, no contemporary records have been unearthed to substantiate the alleged deed.

Ellsworth's remaining months as a cattle town were marked by several more killings. Cad Pierce, a Texan and a friend of Ben Thompson, was killed by policeman Ed Crawford who provoked him into a fight, and some months later Crawford was murdered in a brothel by unknown assailants, but it was believed that they were Texans. Morco was fired from the police force and left town, but months later he came back and was killed by the new marshal, J. Charles Brown, when he refused to remove a pair of ivory-butted six-shooters.

Wichita's entry into the cattle trade had begun in the late 1860s, but not until the arrival of the railroad in May 1872 could she compete with her rivals. She was ideally located for trading, being right at the official end of the Chisholm Trail. The town was incorporated in July 1870, and by the following April was classed as a city. Several marshals had been hired and fired during its first three years of existence, and it was not until 13 April 1871, when the council hired Michael Meagher as marshal, that law and order was established. Meagher held the job for five years with only one short break (1874-5) during which time although there was violence he managed to keep it down. During the period he was not serving as marshal, however, things suddenly got out of hand.

William Smith was appointed marshal for 1874-5 and during his reign the Texans took advantage of him, for he was not in the same class as Meagher. Led by the notorious William Martin, known as 'Hurricane Bill', the 'Texas Gang' shot up the town and made life very difficult. Appalled by the furious uproar, someone rang the police alarm. All hell broke loose. Men came running from their homes or stores armed with an assortment of weapons, until more than fifty of them were grouped around the Texans. At that moment Marshal Smith came running up and tried to persuade both groups to disperse, but neither side would back down.

Just when tension seemed at breaking point, a lawyer, S. M. Tucker, stepped out of the crowd and declared that he did not intend to waste his time – did the marshal want someone arrested and if so whom? Smith nodded and pointed at the Texans. 'All right, arrest "Hurricane Bill".' Amid dead silence Tucker swung up the barrels of his shotgun, cocked the weapon and pointed at Bill's stomach. 'Drop those guns,' commanded Tucker. Martin looked at the barrels of the shotgun and then at Tucker's determined face. He shrugged his shoulders and handed over his pistols. 'I guess you can have me,' he said. Dumbfounded the rest of the gang followed suit and were all jailed.

Wyatt Earp served on the Wichita police force during 1875 and the early part of 1876, but never became marshal. The family had apparently been in the city since early 1874, because in the May of that year Bessie Earp, the wife of Wyatt's brother James, was fined in the Wichita police court for being a prostitute, as was Sallie Earp who lived with her, although

GOVERNOR'S PROCLAMATION.

WHEREAS, C. B. Whitney, Sheriff of Ellsworth County, Kansas, was murdered in the said county of Ellsworth, on the 15th day of August, 1873, by one William Thompson, said Thompson being described as about six feet in height, 26 years of age, dark complexion, brown hair, gray eyes and erect form; and Whereas, the said William Thompson is now at large and a fugitive from justice;

NOW THEREFORE, know ye, that I, Thomas A. Osborn, Governor of the State of Kansas, in pursuance of law, do hereby offer a reward of **FIVE HUNDRED DOLLARS** for the arrest and conviction of the said William Thompson, for the crime above named.

L. S.

IN TESTIMONY WHEREOF, I have hereunto subscribed my name, and caused to be affixed the Great Seal of the State. Done at Topeka, this 22d day of August, 1873.

THOMAS A. OSBORN.

By the Governor:
W. H. SMALLWOOD, Secretary of State.

it is not certain what their relationship was. Both women were fined $8 each and $2 costs. During the next eighteen months a number of similar fines were imposed on the two women and several other ladies named 'Earp' but their relationship with Wyatt is uncertain.

When Dodge City assumed the mantle of 'Queen of the Cowtowns' in 1874 she had already started shipping cattle east but not in large numbers. Now she was the principal shipping point. Law, after a fashion, came in November 1872 when Billy Brooks, the erstwhile marshal of Newton, was hired. His position was not legal because the newly born town was still not incorporated; this came about on 7 March 1874, by which time Brooks was long gone. Billy Brooks, or 'Bully' Brooks as he was also known, had fallen out with a buffalo hunter named Kirk Jordan who had lain in wait for him with a buffalo rifle. Someone warned Brooks who just managed to jump behind two water butts before the huge slug from Jordan's rifle slammed into them. Fortunately for Billy it was deflected by an iron hoop. Billy's pistol had stuck in its holster, and before Jordan could reload he was up and running. He remained hidden in a livery stable until friends of both men persuaded them to meet and shake hands.

Brooks left Dodge shortly afterwards and was later reported in various locations. One story alleged that he had been killed in a gunfight with Morgan Earp in 1877, but his most likely end was in July 1874, when a number of horse-thieves were lynched in Sumner County, Kansas, among them a certain 'W. L. Brooks'.

The first official marshal of Dodge City was Lawrence E. Deger (not Matt Dillon as some suppose). He was appointed in the spring of 1876 and remained in office until 4 December 1877, when he was replaced by Edward J. Masterson, the elder brother of Bat Masterson. At that time Bat was sheriff of Ford County, so between them the brothers were the 'law' in that part of Kansas.

As a policeman Edward Masterson was diligent, courageous and popular with most of the citizens. It was said of Ed that he never shirked his duty and

92
An alleged photograph of Billy Brooks, ex-stage driver, marshal and finally horse-thief, the doubt being that he appears to be armed with a Colt Model 1873 'Army' revolver, not available when Brooks died in 1874. As it is the only one in existence, Billy Brooks it remains.

never stepped away from a fight. In November 1877, when assistant marshal, he was wounded in a fracas trying to prevent a shoot-out between two Texans. His wound was not serious and the local press paid tribute to his 'pluck and nerve', and by the time he became marshal, his reputation was growing daily.

On the night of 9 April 1878, Ed disarmed a Texan named Jack Wagner and gave his pistol to the man's boss, A. M. Walker. Shortly afterwards, in company with deputy marshal Nat Hayward, Ed again found Wagner armed. Ed stepped forwards to disarm him, and Wagner's friends, who were also drunk, rushed out of the saloon. Hayward moved in to assist and was confronted by two armed Texans who threatened to shoot if he interfered. One of them, said to be Walker, actually pulled the trigger of his pistol, but fortunately it misfired. At that moment Wagner thrust his pistol into Masterson's stomach and fired. The heavy lead ball rocked Ed on his feet and the flash of flame from the black powder set his clothing on fire. Yet despite his terrible wound, Ed managed to pull his pistol and immediately shot Wagner and Walker who had interfered.

Bystanders rushed to the marshal's assistance and the other Texans were arrested. Ed meantime brushed off their help and walked slowly across the street to George M. Hoover's saloon, somehow climbed the steps to the sidewalk and entered the door. He stood for a moment swaying on his feet and then said to the bartender, George Hinkle: 'George, I'm shot.' He sank to the floor. Someone rushed forward and smothered the fire in his clothing and he was carried upstairs to his brother Bat's room. Despite his terrible wound and the agony, he remained calm and died bravely within half an hour.

It has been alleged that Bat Masterson was on the street when the shooting commenced and that it was he and not Ed who shot Wagner and Walker, while still on the run, but the contemporary press makes no mention of Bat except to note that he was the only close relative who attended Ed's funeral the next day.

Wagner died the following day and the Dodge City *Times*

93 and 94
'Bat' Masterson (left) was born in Canada in 1853 and christened Bartholomew, moving to Illinois, then Kansas with his family. This portrait was made in 1878 when he was sheriff of Ford County. Later he became for some reason William Barclay Masterson and, after a hectic career as a lawman, gambler and gunfighter, went East at the turn of the century, becoming a journalist. He died at his desk as a noted sportswriter in 1921. His brother Edward was Marshal of Dodge in 1878, when he was killed. The badge is unusual, but badges were not always the traditional star.

noted that he had recently suffered a fall from his horse 'which it is thought rendered him partially insane'. Alfred Walker's father came up from Texas and had him taken to Kansas City to recover, and then left for Texas after making arrangements for his son to follow. But the old man died at Fort Scott from what the *Times* described as 'something like cramp'.

Dodge City's reign as 'Queen of the Cowtowns' lasted until 1885, but long before then she was challenged in the cattle trade stakes briefly by Brookville, Salina and finally Caldwell. The latter provided the only serious rivalry. Although

95
Dodge City's famous Front Street in the 1880s, with a notice prohibiting the carrying of firearms.

the Texas cattle trade via the Chisholm Trail had passed close to the place, there was little the town could do to benefit because it lacked a railroad link. It was not until 1880 that the railroad came through. As it was, she had to share the trade with her neighbour Hunnewell, otherwise historians believe that Caldwell might well have enjoyed the greatest volume of business of all the Kansas cowtowns.

With the arrival of the cattle trade, violence in Caldwell increased accordingly. Until July 1879, the place was without law and order because it was not incorporated and had suffered the same problems as Abilene had ten years before. But once that was rectified elections were held and on 14 August the office of marshal was created and the first man to fill it was George W. Flatt.

Flat had only recently proved his worth during a riot and he was the obvious choice. He served until 1880 when his place was taken by William Horseman. Evidently Flatt upset a number of people, particularly the police force, and on 19 June 1880 he was gunned down on the streets. Subsequent investigation indicated that the police were responsible, and his successor, Horseman, was later tried for the murder but was acquitted.

Later that year, Frank J. Hunt, a deputy policeman when Flatt was killed, and one of the men implicated in his death, exchanged shots with a cowboy in self-defence and killed his horse. On 8 October he was sitting in the Red Light dance hall sulking over a difficulty he had had with one of the girls and her 'man', when he was shot from outside. He died within a few days. Almost two years later – in the same dance hall – City Marshal George Brown was shot when he and constable Willis Metcalf were looking for a man reported to be carrying a pistol. The two officers were surprised by four men as they mounted the stairs and in the struggle Brown was shot through the head. The murderers escaped but were later captured after a fight, and one of them died from his wounds.

Despite the excessive violence that marked the brief period of the Kansas cattle trade, the casualties did not number the 'thousands' one would expect. Historian Robert R. Dykstra in his book *The Cattle Towns*, published in 1968, listed forty-five homicides that took place in the towns involved during the period 1870–85. Of this number few were the direct result of shoot-outs between the police and the transient cowboys and gamblers. More recent research has indicated that this figure is much higher, particularly in Newton and Dodge City. It was left for fiction writers to increase the numbers a hundredfold.

Yet without policemen there is no doubt that cowtown fatalities would have been much higher, for as we have seen, some men were able to rule without too much bloodshed while others, through no fault of their own, were forced to kill to maintain law and order amid 'cowboy chaos'. Even stripped of his glamour, the cowtown marshal is still a formidable figure.

96
The taller man, looking like a young Joel McCrea, is William 'Bill' Tilghman (pronounced Tyman), the other is his buffalo-hunting friend, James Elder. Tilghman, born in 1854, first achieved fame as an alleged train robber. On 10 April 1884, he was appointed Marshal of Dodge City, with Thomas C. Nixon as his assistant, and was much admired. He became famous soon after settling in Oklahoma Territory in 1889, proving one of the greatest of all lawmen, and by no means a ruthless one. William Doolin, a product of the Dalton gang before achieving his own bunch, once refused to allow his men to kill the unsuspecting Tilghman, saying: 'Bill Tilghman's too good a man to be shot in the back.' Finally, Bill died with his boots on as an old man, being killed as marshal of Cromwell by a drunken prohibition officer.

9 SIX-SHOOTER SHOWDOWNS

If you have to shoot a man, shoot him in the guts near the navel, you may not make a fatal shot, but he will get a shock that will paralyse his brain and arm so much that the fight is all over.
Wild Bill Hickok, 1871

The saloon was crowded. The murmur of voices, the clink of glasses and bursts of laughter interspersed with sounds of music, were suddenly stilled by shouts and the scraping of chairs. Two men jumped to their feet pulled their pistols and began shooting. Suddenly one of them rushed towards the pot-bellied stove in the centre of the room and the other one chased him. Round and round they dashed, still firing. Finally one man fell and the other one was grabbed by the police. And despite the fact that eleven shots were fired nobody else was hurt!

That shoot-out was not a synopsis for a Western film; it actually happened. On 5 April 1879, Levi Richardson, a buffalo hunter credited with being a crack shot and the winner of several gunfights, and a gambler named Frank Loving, known to his friends as 'Cock-Eyed Frank', got into a fight. They had quarrelled before, some said over Richardson's wife, and when the shooting started both men fired indiscriminately. Loving retreated behind the stove pursued by Richardson, still shooting. Loving suddenly stood his ground and calmly shot Richardson in the chest, and as he staggered back fired twice more, hitting him once. Levi Richardson managed to get off one more shot before crashing to the floor, by which time the town marshal, Charles Bassett, and a deputy sheriff had disarmed Loving. They grabbed Richardson's pistol as he tried to raise himself from the floor, then he collapsed and died.

Once the smoke had cleared and the confusion had died down, men picked themselves up off the floor or crawled out from behind the bar, amazed to find that no one apart from the antagonists was injured. Later a jury found that Loving had shot in self-defence following provocation from Richardson. When the pistols of both men were examined Loving's .44 Remington was empty and there was one live round and five empty cartridges in Richardson's six-shooter. Eleven shots and only two hits!

Old-timers mulled over that fight for years. Those who witnessed it were amazed at its outcome. Richardson for once had forgotten the golden rule of gunfighting: 'Take your time, place your shots, keep calm and don't lose your nerve.' Bat Masterson took the argument a stage further when, in 1907, he wrote in *Human Life*:

> In asking me to offer an opinion on the question of physical courage as exemplified by them [man-killers] under nerve-trying conditions, he [the editor] has placed a responsibility on my shoulders that I hardly care to assume. I have known so many courageous men in that vast territory lying west and south-west of the Missouri River – men who would when called upon face death with utter indifference as to consequences, that it would be manifestly unjust for me even to attempt to draw a comparison.

Bat went on to claim that courage alone was not enough and that two other qualities were required:

> Any man who does not possess courage, proficiency in the use of fire-arms, and deliberation had better make up his mind at the beginning to settle his personal differences in some other manner than by an appeal to the pistol. I have known men in the West whose courage could not be questioned and whose expertness with the pistol was simply marvellous, who fell easy victims before men who added deliberation to the other two qualities.

That most of the men who

97

A far cry from Wild Bill Hickok's dangerous days and nights in Abilene. He is seen here with Texas Jack Omohundro (centre) and Buffalo Bill Cody (right) when appearing with Buffalo Bill's Combination in 1873. However, the bright lights and false heroics did not appeal to Hickok and he left the show in 1874. It should be stressed that he was appearing in a 'play': the great days of Cody's Wild West Show had yet to come (1883).

engaged in gunfights possessed courage and determination is evident, but proficiency with firearms varied from man to man. Since the gun is the symbol and the instrument that gave him purpose, this is the moment to examine some of the better known weapons and compare their capabilities.

By far the most popular revolver was the Colt which in various forms was in use from 1836 (a year after the first version was patented in England) until the end of the gunfighter era in the early years of this century. The early pistols manufactured at Paterson, New Jersey, by the Patent Arms manufacturing company were equipped with a folding trigger that dropped only when the hammer was pulled back and these early ones did not have a bullet rammer. These five-shot weapons underwent several changes in design and were extremely popular in Texas, where, following some use by the Texas Navy (at that time she was still a Republic), they were issued to the Texas Rangers who used them to good effect against marauding Comanches.

In 1846 Samuel Colt produced a new pistol. Following advice from Captain Samuel Walker, a former Texas Ranger, Colt redesigned the action and the new pistol had a conventional triggerguard, an attached rammer and it was now a six-shooter. These huge .44 calibre pistols weighed more than four pounds, and with a charge of fifty grains of black powder could despatch a lead ball more than six hundred yards with an initial muzzle velocity of 1500 feet per second!

Unfortunately, the weapon was too powerful and some of them blew up.

Colt next designed a 'Dragoon' or 'Army' revolver which is known to modern collectors as the '1848 Dragoon'. This weapon weighed just a little less than the Colt-Walker and the charge was dropped to forty grains. It proved to be a very popular weapon with mounted troops and with several modifications remained in production until 1873, but it was never liked by gunfighters.

Several pocket pistols were also produced, but it was the appearance late in 1850 of a new 'ranger size pistol' that was of particular interest to the gun-toting fraternity. This weapon weighed just over two pounds unloaded, was six-shot, .36 calibre and extremely accurate. The United States Navy Board conducted some trials and as a result the weapon was renamed and today is called 'Colt's Navy revolver, model of 1851' – a pistol that survived until the late 1870s and is one of the most prized and most copied of all Colt's pistols.

In California the demand for the 'Navy' was such that Sam Colt had to put on a night shift to cope with it, and in Europe, too, where it was exhibited at the Great Exhibition in 1851, the demand was just as great. Colt even set up a factory in London where he produced about 40,000 of these pistols and a number of pocket pistols. During the Crimean War the British government bought many thousands of 'Navies' thus making the weapon the first revolver to be officially adopted into the British Army and Navy.

During the savage Kansas-Missouri Border wars sales of the 'Navy' were very high, and by the Civil War more than 100,000 of them had been made (and sold) at the Hartford factory alone. Tests of the 'Navy' by both the British and American governments revealed that it was very effective at distances ranging from twenty-five to as much as 400 yards; but like all revolvers, it was rarely used at long distance, and was relied upon more as a close-range weapon.

The 'Navy' was followed in 1860 by the New Model 'Army' revolver, a stream-lined weapon that combined the hard-hitting power of the 'Dragoon' with the lightness and balance of the 'Navy'. A new version of the 'Navy' was also produced in 1861, but was never as popular as the 1851 model.

Sam Colt himself died in 1862 and it was to be another ten years before the most famous of all the pistols that bears his name was produced and put on trial – the now legendary Single Action Army revolver, model of 1873, better known as the 'Peacemaker'. In the .44-40 calibre (a .44 bullet backed by 40 grains of black powder) it was known as the 'Frontier Six-Shooter'.

Following its 1872 trials the pistol was officially adopted a year later by the United States Army, first for cavalry use and later as an Artilleryman's side arm. But its greatest popularity was in the West where it became the favourite of almost every gunfighter. Production of this remarkable old warrior officially stopped in 1941, but in 1956 in response to public demand, it was reintroduced and is still available.

The mechanism of the 'Peacemaker' is identical to all its famous predecessors and is simple and easily adapted to the sort of refinements that gunfighters thought necessary to increase their own and the weapon's efficiency. The hammer controls the movement of the cylinder. Each time it is pulled back by the thumb the cylinder turns, and as the next loaded chamber lines up with the barrel it is locked in position by a 'bolt' or stud which projects through the frame of the pistol and slots into a notch cut into the periphery of the cylinder. The trigger, meantime, engages with a notch cut into the face of the hammer holding it poised until the trigger is pulled. Some gunfighters either took the trigger out entirely or tied it back to the trigger-guard so that the pistol could be worked by the thumb only. Others preferred simply to ease the whole action so that little effort was required to cock and fire the piece, and so gain an edge over their opponents.

On the question of safety, Wyatt Earp's semi-fictional biography by Stuart Lake makes the point that gunfighters normally carried their pistols loaded with only five bullets and let the hammer rest in the empty chamber. This was true, but evidently on one occasion Mr Earp forgot his own advice. In the Wichita *Beacon* of 12 January 1876, it was reported that several days before, as policeman Earp and several of his cronies were sitting in the back room of the Custom House Saloon:

> . . . his revolver slipped from its holster and in falling to the floor the hammer which was resting on the cap, is supposed to have struck the chair, causing a discharge of one of the barrels [chambers]. The ball passed through his coat, struck the north wall then glanced off and passed out through the ceiling. It was a narrow escape and the occurrence got up a lively stampede from the room. One of the demoralised was under the impression that some one had fired through the window from the outside.

Rivalling the Colt pistols were the Remington arms and those of Smith and Wesson. Each in its turn had merit and found favour among gunfighters, cowboys, outlaws, and lawmen alike. We now know that by 1874 John Wesley Hardin was armed with one or a pair of .44 Smith and Wesson

GUN CARE

It has been claimed that many cowboys rarely bothered to clean their six-shooters and that they grew rusty from disuse, but it is unlikely that this was true. Living as they did in a rapidly changing climate and with ever present dust and sand to contend with, Westerners generally took great care of their weapons. In the days of salt-laden black powder which attracted moisture, gunfighters in particular regularly checked the loads in their weapons. One old-timer recalled seeing Wild Bill Hickok empty his cap and ball six-shooters, carefully clean out the chambers, and push a pin through the nipples until, by holding the cylinder at eye level, he could see daylight through the rear of each chamber. He then carefully loaded each chamber with powder, rammed home the lead balls, and finally inspected each copper cap (filled with fulminate of mercury) before placing it on the nipple. Asked if his guns had got damp he looked up in surprise: 'No, but I ain't ready to go yet, and I am not taking any chances – when I draw and pull I must be sure!'

Few men neglected these basic rules and the slightest hint of dust, dirt and damp was carefully obliterated – no more so than the time when the deputy marshal of Caldwell, Dan Jones, suffered an embarrassing moment in a local hotel in 1879. But perhaps we had best let the editor of the Caldwell *Post* explain what happened. In his issue of 25 September he remarked that Dan had a sudden problem:

It happened at one of Caldwell's fashionable hotels, [which,] like all other fashionable hotels, has two small rooms – over each door is an inscription by which a person may know whether he is to be admitted or not, but it being dark, and Dan's 'business' qualifications not allowing him to stop and read everything that is hung up entered. About this time a lady attempted to enter but was foiled by Dan turning an inside latch – the lady hastened away, but soon returned with the key – (this is not a romance) – locked, unlocked and relocked and finally left to return no more.

Now as Dan's occupation calls him on the street he concluded that he might depart with safety, but imagine his feelings when he discovered that he had been locked in, but as will be seen, Dan is equal to all emergencies, and began trying to extricate himself from his odorous prison. There is a seat in the room just opposite the door upon which Dan sat himself down, put his feet against the door, and with Heenan like strength pushed the door asunder, and at the same instant back went Dan's revolver down, down to the bottomless – after which a light was brought into requisition – it was fished up, a tub of water, barrel of soft soap and scrubbing-brush were readily used up and the pistol looks as natural as ever, and if the street gossip don't mention this we will never say a word about it to Dan.

'American' revolvers, and there is some evidence that even Wild Bill may have owned a pair. The attraction was the break-open action (similar to the Webley) and the metallic ammunition. Some men engaged in gunfights with rifles and even shotguns, but the revolver predominated.

The marksmanship of various gunfighters has been argued over for many years. Tests have proved that a man like Wild Bill Hickok *could* hit two foot circles at 100 yards, as has been claimed; he *could* hit two telegraph poles seventy-five feet apart firing two pistols from a point midway between; and he *could* drive the cork through the neck of a whiskey bottle with a .36 calibre bullet without breaking the neck; but how much he actually accomplished is open to doubt because contemporary evidence is lacking. However, it was accepted by his contemporaries that he was a great pistol shot.

Most gunfighters during the percussion period carried their pistols in leather holsters slung on their hips or sometimes waist high with the butts pointing forward for a cross or the plainsman's twist draw – the hand dropped to the butt, the thumb curled over the hammer, and as the pistol was pulled forward and spun into line the thumb cocked it in one movement. Later, when cartridge pistols appeared on the scene and loops were attached to the belts to carry cartridges, it became common to wear the pistol with the butt to the rear as is the practice in most present day Westerns. Unlike the modern 'pistoleer', however, the pistols were not worn low down on the leg but high on the hip. When needed, the old-timers could get at them fast enough, for they were more concerned with survival than speed and the spectacular – that first 'placing shot' often meant life or death, so they could ill afford to rush it.

In the Old West gunfights were the ultimate in personal combat; but few of them bore much resemblance to the legendary face to face confrontation. Hickok's long distance shootout with Tutt in Springfield, Missouri, in 1865, which was mentioned earlier, was an exception; far more common was the close-up encounter such as he had with Philip Coe, a Texas gambler in Abilene on the night of 5 October 1871.

The cattle season was almost over, but some of the Texans had lingered on in and around the town to visit the Dickinson County Fair. On the 5th the weather had been bad, and as the evening came on a number of them made the rounds of the saloons and spent some time in the very few remaining brothels open in the red light district across the tracks. During the evening Hickok meandered around noting that as many as fifty Texans were carousing in various saloons, and he was told that they were forcing people to buy drinks, and even carrying some of them into the bars for the purpose. One report claims that Hickok himself was similarly approached, but 'treated' the boys on the understanding that they kept guns out of it and behaved properly.

At about 9 pm he was in the Novelty Bar having a farewell drink with his friend Michael Williams, an ex-bartender from Kansas City who had spent the summer in town, during which time he had been employed in various capacities in the saloon business. He had just finished a stint as a 'bouncer' for the Novelty Theatre 'policing' the Texans who tried to get past the stage door. Now Mike was preparing to catch the night train to Kansas City. He and Wild Bill had just toasted each other when there was a shot from outside the Alamo Saloon.

'Stay here, Mike,' Hickok is reported to have said, 'I'll handle this.' He then hurried away and came through the rear door of the Alamo Saloon and quickly made his way out to the ornate glass front doors where he was confronted by an armed crowd led by the six foot four inch Phil Coe, gun in hand. 'Who fired that shot?' demanded Hickok. Coe said that he did and explained that it was at a dog. Wild Bill was not convinced, for he had been warned that Coe meant to kill him 'before the frost'. Hickok and Ben Thompson, Coe's former partner, had not got along too well, and there were rumours that when Thompson returned to Texas Wild Bill and Coe had fallen out on several occasions, one reason being allegations by Texans and townsfolk alike that Coe ran a crooked place. There were also unconfirmed reports that they had also had a fight over a prostitute, but whatever the cause, both men were now primed and ready for action.

The presence of the armed group was in open defiance of city ordinances against firearms and his own orders, and Hickok was very angry. He told them to disarm and to leave town. At that moment Coe pointed his pistol at Hickok, and Wild Bill, 'as quick as thought' according to the press, pulled his 'Navies' and fired. But even as he pulled the triggers another man came between him and Coe and took both balls, dropped the pistol he was carrying and fell in the street. Coe fired twice, one shot going between Hickok's legs striking the ground, and the other through his coat tail. Wild Bill stood firm and fired two more shots at Coe, hitting him twice in the stomach.

One of Coe's shots is believed to have hit someone in the crowd, and even as he fell Hickok had turned on them and shouted: 'If any of you want the balance of these pills, come and get them.' The mob stood paralysed, suddenly sober and silent. 'Now every one of you mount his pony and ride for his camp and do it damn quick!' Within five minutes the place was practically deserted. Only then did Hickok take a look at the men he had shot. Coe was in a bad way and was carried to a house near the local school where doctors attended him. But the other man was dead. It was Michael Williams.

Men said that tears ran down Hickok's face as he carried Williams' body into the Alamo and laid it on a billiard table. In the poor light of the street lamps he had committed the one mistake that all policemen dread – he had killed an innocent bystander, although in the circumstances Williams had been armed and apparently a potential enemy. But it did not lessen Hickok's grief or his swift and terrible reaction. Like a tornado he tore through the saloons and cleared them all, and within half an hour Abilene was like a ghost town. It was Hickok who arranged for the shipment of his friend's body back to Kansas City, and he also paid all the funeral expenses.

Phil Coe lingered on in great agony until late in the evening of the 8th or early hours of the 9th. His body was then shipped back to Texas and he was buried at Brenham.

Naturally, the old-timers all differed in the manner in which they believed the Hickok-Coe fight was conducted. The Abilene residents with few exceptions reiterated a later comment in the *Chronicle* which said of Coe: 'served him right'. The Texans thought otherwise; some of them claimed that Hickok murdered Coe by shooting him in the back. This conflicts with the coroner's report, and having examined the evidence it seems certain that the Kansas version is the correct one. Certainly, the fight did not damage Hickok's reputation, rather it enhanced it, and his handling of the Texans during his period in office was particularly appreciated by the local press. In concluding his account of the affair, the editor of the *Chronicle* said:

> We hope no further disturbances will take place. There is no use in trying to override Wild Bill, the Marshal. His arrangements for policing the city are complete, and attempts to kill police officers or in any other way create disturbance, must result in loss of life on the part of violators of the law. We hope that all, strangers as well as citizens, will aid by word and deed in maintaining peace and quietness.

For sheer drama, the gunfight at Holbrook, Arizona, between the Blevins gang and Commodore Perry Owens is unequalled in the annals of the West. It happened in 1887 during Arizona's Pleasant Valley war, an even more murderous feud than the Lincoln County war, but it was only incidentally part of the war which raged between the Grahams and the Tewksburys, described in Chapter 2.

The little town of Holbrook on the afternoon of 4 September 1887, was remarkably quiet for a place that was notorious for being wild and woolly. The only exciting thing to happen so far that day had been the appearance of a noted cattle thief, Andy Blevins, known in Arizona as Andy Cooper, in a saloon where he boasted how he had killed a Tewksbury and another man two days earlier. Then he headed for his mother's home.

That afternoon, Commodore Perry Owens, the new sheriff of Apache County, rode into town on official business, and the citizens were more than somewhat startled by their first sight of him, especially those who had hoped for law and order. He left his horse at Brown and Kinder's Livery Stable, then started to look the town over. Few people that day knew that he was a tough product of rugged cattle drives out of Texas, and the sight of him was not encouraging.

The trouble was that he did not look right for the 1880s. His hair trailed down below his

98
Sheriff Commodore Perry Owens, who marched up to a house in Holbrook, Arizona, in 1887, to take in a horse thief and found himself confronting a whole family of killers. In a single lethal minute he killed three, wounded a fourth, and walked away unharmed.

shoulders reminiscent of Wild Bill Hickok a decade or more before, and his face was singularly unlined and pleasant to behold. He wore chaps that were decorated with ornaments beyond useful requirement, a large gaudy sombrero, and his Colt .45 was worn on his left hip, butt forward, in the style of the old-time cap and ball pistols. But his Winchester somehow suggested something more than a dude – that and the way the tall and wiry-looking young man carried himself, and the determined look on his face. Dude he may have seemed, but Owens was as tough and as good a shot as any of the tougher-looking individuals who opposed him.

His extraordinary name had been foisted upon him by his romantically-minded father, an ardent admirer of the old naval hero, Commodore Perry.

Owens's arrival in town that day was not by chance. He was aware that Andy Cooper was in the vicinity and had decided to come in and if possible arrest him, not for his participation in the Pleasant Valley war, but for stealing Navajo horses.

Andy's alias was due to a little matter of murder in Texas. His arrival in Holbrook had been welcomed not only by his mother, but by a whole galaxy of Blevins talent, for in the house was his brother Johnny and kid brother, sixteen-year-old Houston. His brother-in-law, Mose Roberts was also there together with Johnny's wife, a Mrs Gladden and her nine-year-old daughter.

Johnny had seen the sheriff arriving at the livery stable and had rushed to alert Andy. He, too, had seen Owens ride in and the pair headed for home. Owens cleaned his six-shooter, but while he was doing it, a local sheepman and politician alerted him that Andy Blevins was preparing to leave town. He hastily reassembled his pistol, grabbed his Winchester and left the stable, giving instructions for his horse to be ready for him. Just before Owens rode up, Johnny Blevins had been mending his violin there.

The events which followed would have made a classic film script but, apart from some coverage in Earle R. Forrest's *Arizona's Dark and Bloody Ground*, (1936) they have received little publicity.

Owens walked towards the nearby house, which stood fifteen feet back from the street, and as he approached, he saw Andy Blevins or as he preferred to be called, Cooper, rapidly saddling a horse, only to bolt indoors when he saw the advancing sheriff. Owens walked up onto the porch and saw Cooper and three other men through a window. He ordered Cooper to come out and, moments later, the rustler slowly opened the door with his left hand and faced the sheriff with a pistol in his right. At the same moment, Johnny Blevins opened the side door off the porch to Owens's right, placing him between the two armed brothers.

Nearer death than at any time in his eventful career, Owens stared hard at Andy Cooper, knowing that if he took his eyes off him for an instant he would have been a dead man. As it was, Cooper's failure to act at once remains a mystery.

'Cooper, I want you,' said Commodore Perry Owens evenly.

'What do you want with me?' asked Andy grimly.

'I have a warrant for you,' replied the sheriff and when Andy, playing for time, asked: 'What warrant?' went on: 'The same warrant for horse-stealing I told you about some time ago.'

Cooper asked him to wait while he saw about it, but Owens had other ideas. 'You must come at once.'

The lightning swift events of the next few minutes were reported in the St Johns *Herald* of 8 September 1887, and at the inquest; the fact that Mrs Blevins and her daughter-in-law later claimed that Andy was unarmed need not detain us here. One can understand their motives, but the idea is fatuous.

'I won't go,' Andy retorted, and fired almost simultaneously with Owens, who was unharmed. Cooper fell back mortally wounded.

Johnny Blevins also fired, missing Owens, but hitting Cooper's horse. Owens swung round, his Winchester still at the hip, and blasted Blevins' back with a shot that hit him in the shoulder.

While Mrs Blevins, who had been by the door, led the dying Cooper into the room, Owens fell back to the street to cover both sides of the house, loosing off a shot at Cooper whom he glimpsed through the window.

Now Mose Roberts joined in the action, leaping through a door or window in the corner of the house, his six-shooter in his hand. Owens's split-second reactions saved him yet again, for he hurled himself to one side of a wagon and fired before Roberts could get his gun into action. He stumbled back into the house, his life ebbing away.

Sheer horror and shock had gripped the remaining inhabitants of the house, but young Sam Houston Blevins, not yet a criminal himself, was not prepared to let his family be killed off unavenged. He tried to grab his brother Johnny's gun, but the wounded man refused to give it up, so he ran to where Andy Cooper lay dying and seized his. Then he charged through the front door, his frantic mother failing to hold him back. Before he could fire, the sheriff's terrible Winchester belched fire yet again and the boy staggered and fell back dead into his mother's arms.

Suddenly all was still except for the weeping women and the groaning of the wounded Johnny Blevins. Commodore Perry Owens stared hard at the house of death, then he walked away leaving the survivors of the clan to mourn their dead in a nightmare atmosphere of blood, pain and anguish. The whole fight had lasted about a minute and only Johnny had survived.

As for Owens, who was thirty-five when he fought his epic battle, from which he emerged unscathed, his career blossomed. The classic photograph of him fits his legend, but, with time and persuasion from his wife, the long hair was clipped to a 'respectable' length, and his clothing became more sober. Owens later became a successful businessman and retired to Seligman, Arizona, where he was the hero of the local small boys – except those who, as small boys will, tried to get 'uppity' with the old man and were chased for their sins. Owens died with his boots off in 1919.

For sheer dogged determination and raw courage, Andrew L. Roberts's last stand at Blazer's Mill has few equals in the annals of the West. It was one of the many highlights of the Lincoln County war (described in Chapter 2), an epic shootout between 'Buckshot' or 'Buckshot Bill' Roberts (his given name appears to have been William) and no less than fourteen men.

Roberts's origins are obscure, or, rather, there are too many contradictory stories about him, as the best account of him, *The Gunfight at Blazer's Mill* by Colin Rickards (1974), shows. But he was certainly a Southerner, and he came to New Mexico around 1875, starting a small ranch on the Rio Ruidoso. Short and shabby, he was nicknamed for a buckshot wound in his right shoulder, though how he got it is unknown. Too crippled to raise a rifle, he shot from the hip – brilliantly, as he proved on his last day on earth, 4 April 1878, when the Lincoln County war had been going on for forty-five days.

Blazer's Mill was on the Mescalero Apache Reservation and was run by Dr Joseph H. Blazer who, after several careers including that of a dentist, then ran a timber business. When the Agency was established, he was allowed to retain his well-run property, which virtually became its headquarters.

There was no reason for Roberts to become involved in the war, but, unfortunately for him, he joined the posse that murdered John Tunstall, a killing that, as we have seen, triggered off the action. He may have needed the posse fee. He was not in the section of Mathews's men that killed the Englishman, but the avenging 'Regulators' were not concerned with such details, and Roberts decided to leave Lincoln County. He sold his property and waited for a cheque for it that was to be sent to the post office run by Dr Blazer.

There is a story that he happened to meet Billy the Kid and Charlie Bowdre and opened fire on them as a safety precaution. They recognised him before they fled. If this indeed happened, Buckshot Roberts had all the more reason to scan each mail delivery. Another story – firmly believed by his opponents – has it that he signed on as a bounty hunter, there being rewards out for the killers of Sheriff Brady and Hindman; but brave (and needy) as he was, this would seem to have been foolhardy.

On 4 April, Roberts was waiting at the main building in the small settlement for the mail carrier. This was a two-storey house built against possible Indian attack, and now part Agency, part restaurant lodging house and trading post. The actual mill was some 250 yards away.

An Apache herder reported that a gang had killed and butchered a steer locally the previous night, and Blazer, guessing who they were, asked Roberts to leave. He agreed, arranging that his cheque should be sent on elsewhere, then he loaded his packhorse with his gear, got on his mule, and rode up a trail through timber to avoid the intruders.

The Regulators reached Blazer's Mill and left their horses in a high corral, then went into the house for a meal. Meanwhile, Roberts, having spotted the mail carrier, rode back, not realising that his enemies had reached the settlement. He left his gunbelt on his saddle horn – Blazer liked weapons 'parked' – and headed for the door on the west of the building.

Regulator Frank Coe, who knew Roberts well, was interviewed nearly half a century later and left an account generally accepted as accurate, allowing for memory lapses, and there were other witnesses of the stirring drama who later spoke, including Frank's cousin George.

It was John Middleton, guarding the saddle horses while the others ate, who reported to Dick Brewer, leader of the Regulators, that 'a mighty well-armed man' was hitching his mule outside, a common enough happening for the rest to continue eating. Frank Coe finished first, went out and saw his friend 'Buckshot' Roberts shaking hands with him and urging him to surrender.

The other diners finished and began to appear; Brewer, a handsome, admirable rancher and employee of Tunstall's, whose death he had taken hard, now restraining his more itchy-trigger-fingered men. The tension grew as the talk between Roberts and Coe continued, then round the corner of the house came John Middleton, Henry Brown, Charlie Bowdre and Frank MacNab closely followed by George Coe. Roberts, who by this time was sitting in the doorway, got up and faced them at fifteen feet.

'Throw up your hands or you are a dead man,' called Bowdre.

'Not much, Mary Ann,' replied Roberts coolly and brought his rifle to his hip to face Bowdre's pistol. Both fired and Roberts received an agonising 'gut wound', his own

THE BUNTLINE SPECIAL

Wyatt Earp without his Buntline Special would be like a cowboy without his horse – unthinkable! But . . .

In 1930 readers of the *Saturday Evening Post* were surprised to read, in a series of articles about Wyatt Earp written by Stuart Lake, that in 1876 E. Z. C. Judson, alias Ned Buntline, the legendary dime novelist, had travelled west to Dodge City and presented a number of famous peace officers with special 'Peacemakers' with extra length barrels and wooden carbine stocks with the name Ned carved into them.

Almost overnight Wyatt Earp's Buntline Special became a part of not only Earp's legend but also that of the West. Innumerable old-timers came forward recalling how they had seen Wyatt 'buffalo' (that is, hit over the head) some unruly cowboy, or draw his Buntline from a specially made holster 'almost as fast as most men can jerk a normal six-gun!' It became a 'prop' in the television series devoted to Wyatt Earp that flitted across our screens during the 1950s, and no mention of Wyatt was complete without reference to the Buntline.

But facts are facts. There never was a Buntline Special: Ned Buntline never heard of Wyatt Earp, and for health and other reasons, Buntline was in no position to make a trip to Dodge City in 1876 to bestow 'special' firearms upon a group of peace officers who were hardly known in Kansas, let alone as far away as New York!

Why then did Lake mention it? Earp scholars believe that it was a ploy on his part to create for his hero something different to set him apart from his fellows. Why not a special gun: one of a kind? True, he did claim that Buntline presented five others, but he was also very careful to point out that they all cut their barrels down to regular size, leaving Wyatt's the exception.

It is also true that the Colt Company did (and still do) produce 'Peacemakers' with extra long barrels – 10in, 12in and 16in – which come fitted with a skeleton carbine stock if required. But that is all. Until Lake's disclosure the company had never heard of their weapons being called 'Buntline Specials' and an intensive search of their records found no mention of him or any such order. However, they realised the sales potential of such a gimmick, and today they sell various 'Buntline Specials', thereby perpetuating a myth that would have awed even a publicity seeker like Wyatt into open-mouthed admiration!

bullet shooting off Bowdre's gun-belt. It fell to the ground, while the bullet ricochetted and mangled George Coe's trigger finger and thumb, tearing his pistol from his hand as he fired. He and Bowdre ducked for cover.

The other Regulators began firing, but, amazingly, 'Buckshot' Roberts, himself firing as he retreated along the wall, was not hit. He sent a bullet through John Middleton's lung.

Then his carbine was empty and Billy the Kid rushed him, only to be knocked breathless by Roberts's gun used like a bayonet. The Kid's bullet missed, and Roberts reached the comparative safety of Blazer's office, where he had some luck. His ammunition was gone, his pistol was on his mule, but he found Blazer's Springfield 45-60, plus plenty of bullets. Then he dragged a mattress in front of the half open door, lay on it and commenced firing. He was in agony, but clearly determined to go down fighting.

The Regulators debated attacking Roberts by rushing him or letting him die – in less than three hours guessed Frank Coe. And now a friend of Roberts's, Numa Strain, began trying to work his way towards him. Roberts urged him not to interfere and a threatening Billy the Kid forced him to retreat. He tried to get volunteers to help his friend at the Agency, but nobody stepped forward.

Billy the Kid now ordered Dr Blazer to eject Roberts, but Blazer pointed out that he was as likely to be shot by Roberts as anyone else. Meanwhile, the wounded were being tended by the Indian agent, F. C. Godfroy, the day was getting hotter, and Dick Brewer decided things were getting out of hand. He crept to a position near the saw mill behind a pile of logs. Bowdre may have been with him.

Brewer then fired through the doorway and there was silence. Fatally thinking that Roberts was dead or incapable, Brewer raised himself up for his next shot and received a bullet 'in the middle of the forehead', as Frank Coe recalled, which 'tore off the top of his head . . . it was a great piece of marksmanship', or, perhaps, its perfection was sheer luck, but the result was one of the most famous shots in Western history.

The Regulators had already decided that they must leave and take the wounded to a doctor, and now that Brewer was dead, they headed for Frank Coe's ranch. Meanwhile, Blazer had a hard task convincing the dying 'Buckshot Bill' that his enemies had gone, the heroic cripple having not surprisingly become trigger-happy. Blazer and the family of the Indian agent did their best for him as preparations were rapidly made to bury Brewer, the sun making it vital to do it as soon as possible. Around noon the following day, Roberts, who had been in a coma since dawn, died and was buried beside Brewer, whose death was a serious blow to the fortunes of the Tunstall/McSween faction. Roberts's death was less 'significant', but he occupies a special place in the Western Valhalla, along with Nate Champion of the Johnson County war fame. The lone warrior against massive odds will never lose his appeal.

* * *

Community shoot-outs were less common than Western novels and films suggest, but when such an event occurred the result was disaster. We have already noted Mike McCluskie's action when he killed a Texan named Bailey (or Wilson) in Newton and the threat made on his life by other Texans. McCluskie, however, chose to ignore those threats and despite further warnings returned to defy his enemies.

McCluskie was a hard-headed Frontier 'tough' who had followed the tracks west and at times had been employed as a railroad policeman. He had been in trouble with the authorities on several occasions, but had managed to extricate himself from any really serious consequences. The killing of Bailey, however, was different. The people of Newton could not have cared less if either had been killed, but Bailey's fellow Texans thought otherwise. Led by Hugh Anderson, a friend of John Wesley Hardin, and himself a notorious desperado and killer, the Texans planned their revenge.

McCluskie's return to Newton was carefully noted and a watch was kept on his movements. Late on the night of 19 August he made his way to Perry Tuttle's saloon on the south-west corner of West Second and Popular Streets.

If McCluskie was aware of his peril he foolishly neglected to take precautions to protect himself, or perhaps his contempt for his would-be attackers overcame natural caution. In any event, led by Anderson a group of Texans entered the saloon and one then approached McCluskie. His job was to distract his attention while the others positioned themselves. At that moment Hugh Anderson stepped into view and walked up to McCluskie's table, pistol in hand. 'You are a cowardly son of a bitch! I will blow the top of your head off!' he shouted and fired. His shot went through McCluskie's neck and he tried to rise at the same time pulling and firing his pistol. But the hammer failed to detonate the cap. Desperately he recocked it and by this time he was covered in blood. As he fell to the floor Anderson stepped forward and shot him through the back.

What happened next is still talked about in Newton. The Texans continued to shoot at others in the room, and then suddenly another man appeared as if from nowhere and began shooting at them. By now the room was full of smoke and flame from the muzzles of more than a dozen six-shooters. Screams and cries rent the air and from outside came an excited babble of voices as men and women from all over town rushed to the scene.

Suddenly it was all over. People stumbled out of the room dazed and shaking, and some of them were carrying lead, while others cautiously ventured in and surveyed the carnage. McCluskie was still breathing and was taken to a room upstairs where he soon died. An innocent bystander named John Martin, a Texan not involved with either side, was also fatally wounded when he tried to stop the shooting. Several of the Texans were killed during the fracas and others died later. But who was the 'Avenging Nemesis' who had done most of the shooting when McCluskie was downed? Nobody knows for sure, but about a year later one Theodore F. Price wrote a poem about the 'massacre', *Newton: A Tale of the South-West*, in which it was alleged that it was a consumptive youngster named Riley, befriended by McCluskie, who tried to save and then avenged his benefactor, and promptly disappeared. The Topeka *Commonwealth* described the event as 'worse than Tim Finnegan's wake', and demanded that something be done and quickly about bringing law and order – which, as was shown elsewhere, was prompted more than anything by the 'General Massacre'.

That might have seemed to be the end of the affair except for a curious aftermath. Three years later Anderson died in a gory duel with a man alleged to be McCluskie's brother. The pair fought it out at Medicine Lodge, Kansas. Having first shot each other full of holes they then crawled towards each other and stabbed one another to death!

Less gory but still fascinating was the confrontation between Dallas Stoudenmire, the man who tamed El Paso, and the Manning brothers who ran most of the town's rackets. Stoudenmire, a former Texas Ranger, stood six feet two inches in his socks. He rarely smiled and his granite jaw and pale face offset by hazel eyes and auburn hair set him apart from his more swarthy companions. He was appointed marshal of El Paso following a number of shoot-outs between Texans and Mexicans over alleged rustling and the Rangers had become involved. Several shootings occurred, and in one of them a police constable was killed. Hearing the shots Stoudenmire appeared on the scene and while still on the run cut loose and killed the man responsible.

For some time Stoudenmire's presence kept the lid on the town and he clamped down on some of the saloons' less publicised activities. Even the town roughs kept quiet for fear of what he could do with the two silverplated short-barreled .44 Smith and Wesson No 3 New Model 'American' revolvers which he carried in specially made leather-lined hip pockets.

On 17 April 1881, a former constable and latterly the town drunk named Bill Johnson tried to kill the marshal and his brother-in-law Doc Cummings (who had married Stoudenmire's sister) as they made the rounds of the city. Cummings was along for 'the ride', when Johnson cut loose with a shotgun but missed. Both men immediately fired back and Johnson fell dead with eight bullets in him. At that moment other men started to shoot and Stoudenmire, guns blazing, rushed toward his unknown assailants who turned in a panic and ran off into the night. During the whole fracas Stoudenmire received only one hit – in his boot heel!

Stoudenmire blamed the Mannings for the trouble but could not prove it. For some months an uneasy truce existed, and he was regarded with admiration by the citizens of El Paso who heaped praise and gifts upon him. Then he began

99
Dallas Stoudenmire photographed when he was Marshal of El Paso, Texas. He rarely smiled and when he did it was disarming. This portrait, for all the badge of office on his lapel, gives no indication of how tough and dangerous he could be.

to take to drink. Nobody really knows what happened to Stoudenmire during that period. Suddenly he announced that he was getting married and some felt that at last he would settle down to a domestic existence. But during his absence on honeymoon when James B. Gillett, a deputy marshal, was left in charge (he later became a very famous Texas Ranger) with Cummings to help him, the latter fell out with the Mannings and was shot dead in their Coliseum Saloon.

When Stoudenmire returned he was shocked and very angry. He promptly declared open war on the Mannings. Fearing what might happen, some of the responsible citizens persuaded both factions to sign a 'peace treaty' not to fight. Reluctantly Stoudenmire agreed but the frustration of his position took its toll, and he began drinking again. During his bout with the bottle, Gillett was made marshal, and it was rumoured that Stoudenmire was leaving town anyway. However, when the position of marshal was suddenly declared vacant and another man was suggested for the job, it was Stoudenmire who got it. But it did not last. His best friend was now the bottle and when the city council threatened to cut his salary he resigned and Gillett was hired in his place.

On 18 September 1882, Stoudenmire decided things had gone far enough and that he would confront the Mannings following allegations that he had intended to force them into a fight. Walt Jones, a former policeman and a friend, went along with him to confirm his intentions. In the Coliseum they found two of the Manning brothers, Jim standing beside the bar and his brother 'Doc' Felix playing billiards. Jim went off to get their brother Frank and 'Doc' laid down his cue and came over. He and Stoudenmire soon got involved in a heated argument and both men went for their guns. Jones tried to interfere but Stoudenmire pushed him aside, which was a tactical mistake. It gave 'Doc' time to pull his double-action .44 and shoot Stoudenmire, but fortunately the ball hit his pocket book and a bunch of letters in his right breast pocket. Manning fired again and this time shot Dallas in the left breast.

Dallas staggered back but by now his gun was out and he shot 'Doc' through the right arm above the elbow. 'Doc' dropped his gun and threw himself upon Stoudenmire and, despite his wound, wrapped his arms around him to prevent him from shooting again. The pair locked together, staggered around the saloon in a macabre dance between a giant and a dwarf, until finally they stumbled out into the street. Jim Manning then appeared brandishing a .45. His first shot smashed a barber's pole, but he steadied his aim and the second one hit Stoudenmire in the head. Stoudenmire's grip went slack and, severely shaken, 'Doc pulled himself free from the corpse, and grabbing one of Dallas's pistols went berserk and began to batter the dead man's head, but he was pulled away by bystanders.

The verdict, when the brothers came to trial, was that Jim had killed Stoudenmire to protect his unarmed brother and no further action was taken. Old-timers, however, shook their heads and maintained that Jim Manning's bullet was only the instrument that killed him: Dallas Stoudenmire really destroyed himself when he took to drink.

100
Edward Schieffelin, who discovered the Lucky Cuss Mine and founded the town of Tombstone.

The most publicised gunfight in the Old West was that between the Earps and the Clantons at Tombstone, Arizona, on 26 October 1881. Generally known as the 'Gunfight at the OK Corral' it actually took place in the street nearby. The details surrounding this classic encounter are as controversial today as they were at the time, but the cause and effect that led to that final showdown should be examined.

In 1877 a prospector named Ed Schieffelin discovered a huge silver lode far out in the wilds of Arizona. It was then Apache country and few people dared to get involved with the ferocious warriors without being well armed or in large numbers. Sometime before his discovery, Schieffelin told a friend that he was prospecting for 'stones' (which was a miner's description of quartz), and the man waggishly replied: 'Ed, I reckon the only stone you're gonna find'll be your tombstone!' Schieffelin was so amused by this that when he did make his big strike he named his diggings Tombstone, and by the early part of 1879 the place had become a town.

Like most mining boom towns its early beginnings were lawless. The lure of silver and the place's potential wealth attracted innumerable characters anxious, despite the dangers en route, to get rich quickly. Some worked in the mines, some manipulated cards in saloons, and others found less energetic but perhaps more reckless pursuits by pulling triggers in holdups.

Amongst those drawn to the magnetic spot were Wyatt Earp

and his brothers Virgil and James. Wyatt and James had travelled from Dodge City, where Wyatt had achieved minor notoriety on the local police force. At Prescott they were joined by Virgil who had worked there as a stagecoach driver and part-time sheriff. The brothers, together with assorted wives and mistresses, arrived in Tombstone in December, 1879, and early in 1880 were joined by their other brother, Morgan, the hot-headed member of the family.

Wyatt Earp in 1880 was nothing like the man immortalised by Stuart Lake in his fictionalised biography *Frontier Marshal* published in 1931. He had been married at the age of twenty to a young girl of sixteen who died in a typhus epidemic, and the lady with him in Tombstone, known to some as Mattie Baylock, may or may not have been his wife for no records have yet been found of their marriage. In his earlier days Wyatt had been a buffalo hunter in Kansas and there is evidence that he and a companion had been accused of horse-stealing at Fort Gibson, Indian Territory. Indicted by a grand jury, Wyatt fled before his case came to trial. He appeared in Wichita in 1874, and the following year served for a time on the police force. Problems over the payment to the city treasury of fines collected by him led to upsets with the administration and later he moved on to Dodge City.

In Dodge Wyatt served as an assistant marshal at various periods between 1876 and 1879, and supplemented his income as a gambler in the Long Branch Saloon and took a percentage of the house 'take'.

The arrival of the Earps in Tombstone was not regarded as an event for none of them were well known outside Kansas. James never became involved in the events which followed. Crippled by a Civil War wound, he was a passive individual who rarely got into difficulties. But both Wyatt and Virgil were gun-toters and Wyatt's reputation in Kansas was of a man who would kill if provoked enough.

When the then marshal of Tombstone, Fred White, was killed in October 1880, Virgil, his assistant, arrested his killer one William 'Curly Bill' Brocius, although it is claimed that Wyatt made the actual arrest. It was reported that White grasped the barrel of Curly's pistol and pulled the weapon toward him. Curly still had his finger on the trigger, and the hammer was cocked . . .

Wyatt bought an interest in the Oriental Saloon, and ran a faro table at the Eagle Brewery, a rival saloon. He also found time to work for Wells Fargo and later served as a deputy sheriff of Pima County.

The Earps were joined in Tombstone by John H. Holliday,a tuburcular dentist familiarly known all over the West as 'Doc' Holliday. His career as a practising dentist had taken him to Dodge City where he had renewed his acquaintance with the Earps (he is believed to have known them for many years before they became partners). Few men liked Holliday. His illness aggravated by excessive alcohol made for a mean disposition, and there were those who believed, perhaps with some cause, that he had a death wish. Few were thinking of dentistry when they considered what it would be like to be 'drilled' by 'Doc' Holliday. But he and Wyatt were very close, and it is claimed that once in Dodge City he saved Wyatt's life when he was threatened by a mob of drunken cowboys.

It was reported that there were two Bibles in town, but their presence did not deter the would-be gamblers and womanisers who continued to flock to the place. Two rival newspapers were established, the Tombstone *Epitaph* (which survived until 1975) and the *Nugget*. The *Epitaph* supported the Earps, while the *Nugget* was very critical of their actions.

It was not long before the Earps fell out with the rival faction which consisted of ranchers, cowboys and itinerant rustlers. The ranchers naturally resented the influx of people to what had been a relatively peaceful area (in between Indian wars) and they did not take kindly to the mining population. For their part the Tombstone-ites regarded the ranchers and their cowboy minions as semi-wild anyway, and few of them felt inclined to distinguish between who was a genuine honest cowboy and who a rustler.

The Earps and their followers were right in the middle. Wyatt had little liking for cowboys, hardened as he was to the violence of their Texas cousins. This soon led to a disagreement with the most notorious of the rancher-rustler outfits, the Clantons and the McLaurys.

The combined outfits had been raising and rustling cattle since the early 1870s, but as

101
Wyatt Berry Stapp Earp, from a badly retouched photograph made about 1885.

they also had US Government contracts to feed the Apaches, most of the cattle (stolen from Mexicans) were soon disposed of on reservations. There were three Clanton boys, Ike, a very cunning individual, Phineas, and Billy, but overlording the whole family was Old Man Clanton.

Trouble between the Earps and the Clanton-McLaury faction came when Wyatt lost a prized horse. He traced it to Billy Clanton but was assured that it was all a big mistake. Later, when six mules disappeared from an Army post and Virgil, who was then a deputy US marshal, set off with Wyatt and a detail of soldiers to find them, things got serious. The animals were found at the McLaury ranch and the men were on the point of altering the US brand. Again, it was all a misunderstanding, and the brothers promised to return them to the Army, but when the Earps left, rustlers arrived and stole them: no evidence, no prosecution!

102
Morgan Earp, Wyatt's younger brother, who was killed in a pool-room ambush in March 1882 in Tombstone.

The Earps had their own problems. On 15 March 1881, a Kinnear and Company stagecoach was attacked, and the driver, Bud Philpott, was killed. Thanks to Bob Paul, the shotgun guard, they managed to outrun the bandits. The Earps led one posse and sheriff John Behan, a known friend of the Clantons and McLaurys, led another. A local desperado named Luther King was captured and admitted that he and three other toughs, Bill Leonard, Harry Head and Jim Crane, had been involved. Behan took him to Tombstone and by a curious act of stupidity he was allowed to walk out of jail, mount the nearest horse and escape! The Earps returned to learn of his escape and also some nasty rumours that Holliday had been involved in the robbery, but this was never proved.

It was later claimed that Wyatt tried to bribe Ike Clanton into betraying the three remaining outlaws, but he refused despite an ample reward. As it happened, all three men were killed before any such plan could be put into operation. Leonard and Head were killed in a gunfight in Eureka, New Mexico, and Crane was despatched by Mexican regulars soon afterward.

Virgil Earp, in his capacity as a deputy US marshal, also upset sheriff John Behan when he arrested two of his deputies, Frank Stilwell and Pete Spence, for holding up a stagecoach. As both men were also friends of the Clantons and the McLaurys the incident built up further resentment against the Earp faction.

Meeting Morgan on the street

Frank McLaury openly suggested he step into the street and shoot it out, but Morgan declined. None the less, it was a challenge and could not be ignored.

The situation came to a head on the afternoon of 25 October when Ike Clanton had a run in with 'Doc' Holliday at a lunch counter in one of the saloons. He tried to avoid him but Doc would not let him. 'You damn son of a bitch of a cowboy', he sneered, and told him to get himself a gun and get to work. Doc also accused him of threats against his friends the Earps but Ike denied them. Morgan who was in the place stepped forward, and Ike, fearful that there would be shooting, stepped quickly outside. 'Go get heeled!' taunted Doc. At that moment Wyatt and Virgil appeared, and seconds later Morgan came out to the street. Clanton backed off repeatedly denying any intention to fight and, begging Morgan not to shoot him in the back, he scuttled off.

After an all-night session of poker and booze, Ike stepped onto the streets of Tombstone in a belligerent mood, mouthing threats. Wyatt was awakened and informed that Ike had said: 'As soon as those damned Earps make their appearance on the street today, the ball will open.' Wyatt wasted no time and hurried over to the Oriental Saloon where he was told that Ike now had a rifle and a six-shooter. He immediately went to find Virgil and the pair of them separated and set out to find Ike. Virgil found him in an alley.

Ike hardly knew what hit him. Virgil came up to him from behind and grabbed his rifle, and as Ike tried to pull his six-shooter, Virgil hit him over the head with the barrel of his own pistol and Ike collapsed to his knees, shaking his head.

Virgil stood over him. 'I understand you have been hunting for me?' Ike glared up at him. 'If I'd seen you a second sooner I'd have killed you!' Virgil dragged him to his feet and told him he was under arrest for carrying firearms within city limits. As they set off for the court house Morgan appeared and tagged along. Ike was waiting to be led into court when Wyatt came up to him and told him that he had threatened his life once too often and called him a 'dirty cow thief', adding 'if you're anxious to fight, I'll meet you'.

Wiping away the blood that still trickled down his face from Virgil's pistol whipping, Ike told Wyatt that he would see him when he was through in court; 'all I want is four feet of ground'.

The Earps offered to pay his fine if he would fight, but he said he did not need that kind of encouragement. 'I'll fight you anywhere, or any way.'

Judge A. O. Wallace fined Ike $25 for carrying a concealed weapon and as Ike left the court he had another row with Morgan. Meanwhile, outside, Wyatt was having difficulty with Tom McLaury. He ended up by laying the barrel of his pistol alongside Tom's head and leaving him lying in the street glassy-eyed and moaning.

The long awaited and dreaded moment had finally arrived.

Already aware that the Clantons were determined to kill them, the Earps assumed that their recent trouble with Ike Clanton and Tom McLaury was but a preliminary to the main event, and when someone warned them that Ike and Billy Clanton had been joined by the two McLaurys and Billy Claiborne down at the OK Corral, they quickly set off to have it out.

On the way Wyatt and Morgan were joined by 'Doc' Holliday. Wyatt tried to keep him out of it, but Holliday refused. He carried his shotgun, which some writers maintain he had been given only moments before by Virgil, but more recent evidence suggests it was probably the gun he personally ordered from the Birmingham gunmaker, W. W. Greener, to be made up to his own specifications.

Sitting in a barber shop on Allen Street, Sheriff John Behan could see a crowd gathering on the corner. Hearing of the cause he hastened over to the Hafford saloon where he met Virgil who explained the position. Behan asked him to disarm rather than fight the boys: it was his duty to do so. Virgil ignored him so Behan said he would disarm them himself.

He came upon Morgan and 'Doc' Holliday who were soon joined by Virgil, and on the corner of Fremont Street he met Frank McLaury who was holding a horse. Frank said he did not want trouble but that he would not give up his guns, and still talking he and Behan walked towards Fly's Photographic Gallery. Outside were Ike and Billy Clanton, together with Tom McLaury and Billy Claiborne. Behan again tried to get them to disarm, and Ike said that he did not have any guns, opening his coat so that Behan could search him and prove it. Tom McLaury did the same to show that he, too, was unarmed.

Behan asked the others to give up their guns. 'Only if you disarm the Earps,' Frank McLaury replied.

Billy Clanton was now impatient. All morning he had been trying to get the others to leave. 'I want to go home,' he said, repeatedly, adding that he had not come to town to fight. Billy Claiborne shrugged and said he was not really involved at all but was merely trying to get them all to leave town.

Thinking perhaps that he had averted a shoot-out, Behan asked them all to come down to his office, but at that moment the Earps appeared, walking slowly in line abreast and fully armed. 'Stay here,' he said and hurried up to Virgil.

'For God's sake, don't go down there', he begged.

Virgil pushed him aside. 'I'm going to disarm them.' He and his brothers and Holliday then started forward.

Behan rushed after them. 'Go back! I'm sheriff of this county!' he yelled, but the group ignored him.

103
John 'Doc' Holliday, the 'gunfighting dentist' born in 1852. He died of tuberculosis in 1887.

Virgil was careful to legalise their action for he had deputised his brothers and 'Doc' as assistant city marshals. Nevertheless, as the band set off on that last walk it was Wyatt who dominated. Each man was dressed in the long frock coat popularly known as a Prince Albert. From beneath his, Wyatt drew his pistol and slipped it into a specially lined pocket. The coat was new and the tailor had been instructed to make the lining of canvas and to wax-rub it so that a pistol could be pulled at speed. The actual weapon used by Wyatt that day is disputed. Some authorities claim that he was using a .44 8 inch barreled Smith and Wesson 1869 'American' (a gift from his friend John Clum, editor of the *Epitaph*); while others believe it was a Colt Single Action 'Army' .45 – but not the 'Buntline Special' credited to him by his biographer.

As noted earlier, the actual fight took place not in or at the OK Corral but on Fremont Street right in front of C. S. Fly's home and photographic gallery. The Clantons and McLaurys were lined up with their backs against a private home owned by William Harwood as the Earps drew up to within about six or eight feet of them. 'Doc' Holliday remained on the street as the brothers advanced into the vacant lot nearby to bring them into line with the Clantons and McLaurys.

For a moment there was complete silence. Behan had meanwhile slipped off behind Fly's house where he was hastily joined by Billy Claiborne. Later Behan was to testify that he thought Wyatt started the fight when he said: 'You sons of bitches, you have been looking for a fight, and now you can have it.' For his part Wyatt alleged that when Virgil ordered them to give up their guns Billy Clanton and Frank McLaury dropped their hands to their pistols and Virgil then shouted: 'Hold, I don't mean that; I have come to disarm you.'

Billy Clanton shouted out: 'Don't shoot me, I don't want to fight,' and Tom McLaury opened his coat to show he was not armed and said as much. Wyatt later claimed that since Behan had said that he had disarmed the bunch, the sight of pistols in the hands of Frank McLaury and Billy Clanton led him to think otherwise, so he pulled his own pistol. He ignored Billy but shot at Frank whom he regarded as a deadly shot and dangerous. Two shots sounded as one: Wyatt shooting at Frank and Billy Clanton shooting at Wyatt. 'I don't know which shot was fired first. We fired almost together. The fight then became general,' declared Wyatt.

At this point Virgil ordered them back to the street where they joined Holliday. Ike Clanton panicked and rushed up to Wyatt and grabbed his left arm. Seeing he was unarmed Wyatt told him: 'The fight has now commenced; go to fighting, or get away,' and pushed him aside. Ike turned blindly away and ran off eventually reaching the OK Corral and safety, narrowly escaping a blast from Holliday's shotgun.

Wyatt's first shot had hit Frank McLaury in the stomach, but he managed to get one shot off before staggering off towards the street. Tom McLaury, realising that his plea of neutrality was wasted, grabbed his brother's Winchester rifle from its saddle scabbard and took cover behind the horse.

Morgan Earp meantime put a ball into Billy Clanton's right wrist and another in his chest. He fell back against Fly's Gallery and tried desperately to use his pistol. Suddenly, Frank McLaury's horse, frightened by the noise and confusion, reared away and exposed Tom McLaury. Holliday swung the muzzle of his shotgun and fired the remaining barrel. The blast all but knocked Tom off his feet as the buckshot tore into his waistcoat, peppering it with shot holes that rapidly became bloodied. He screamed, staggered back, stumbled into Fremont Street, collapsed and died.

Virgil had so far not fired a shot, but he was soon to learn that Billy Clanton was far from dead. Somehow the dying boy found strength to steady his pistol and put a ball into Virgil's calf knocking him to the ground. Frank McLaury, all but dead, managed to raise his six-shooter and fired it at Doc Holliday. Doc had just thrown down his now empty shotgun and plucked a nickel-plated six-shooter from his pocket. Both Holliday and McLaury fired simultaneously and unobserved by either of them, Morgan Earp also fired at McLaury. Doc missed but Morgan's bullet hit the dying man in the head. McLaury's final shot had nicked Holliday's hip taking a piece of skin and holster with it.

At that moment Billy Clanton also fired his last shot. It hit Morgan Earp in the shoulder, and even as he stumbled and fell, both he and Wyatt fired simultaneously and Billy Clanton hit the ground to rise no more.

There were no further shots. Clouds of white smoke from the black powder loads hung on the still air, and the silence was almost deafening. Suddenly Camillus Fly, armed with a Henry rifle, rushed out of his house and disarmed the still breathing Billy Clanton. As Fly eased the six-shooter out of his hand, the boy's last words were: 'Give me some more cartridges.'

The fight lasted less than a minute, and during that time eight men had diced with death; three of them were dead, three badly wounded, and two survived miraculously without a scratch – Ike Clanton who had turned and run, and Wyatt Earp.

The aftermath of that fight is as controversial as the event. Virgil and Morgan were found to be unfit to stand trial, and Holliday was not called either. But Wyatt was in court and was allowed to read a prepared statement. The hearing lasted thirty days, at the end of which the Earps were exonerated inasmuch as it was felt by the court that their actions had been justified. None the less, Justice Spicer found reason to criticise

Virgil's action in enlisting his brothers' and Holliday's aid in attempting to arrest the Clantons and McLaurys, but added that the social climate then prevailing left Virgil with little choice.

Then, as now, feeling ran high, and some weeks later Virgil was crippled for life when someone emptied a load of buckshot into his side as he left the Oriental Saloon. Morgan, too, became a victim, shot through the back in Hatch's saloon as he played pool in March 1882.

Wyatt suspected Morgan's death was the work of Pete Spence and Frank Stilwell but he was unable to prove it. Wyatt accompanied Virgil and James as far as Tucson when Morgan's body was sent back to their parents' home in California for burial. While the brothers waited for the train to leave, Wyatt came face to face with Frank Stilwell. The Earps later claimed that he had tried to kill Wyatt. At least that is their story. When the train left for California a very dead Frank Stilwell lay on the tracks beside the Union Pacific Depot, six bullets in his body, and powder burns on his clothing. Soon afterwards, Wyatt and 'Doc' Holliday were in the hills on the trail of Pete Spence. He escaped their wrath but a Mexican woodcutter (sometimes described as an Indian) was killed at Spence's camp up in the Dragoons. The Earps then moved on to Albuquerque, New Mexico, leaving behind a reputation both good and bad.

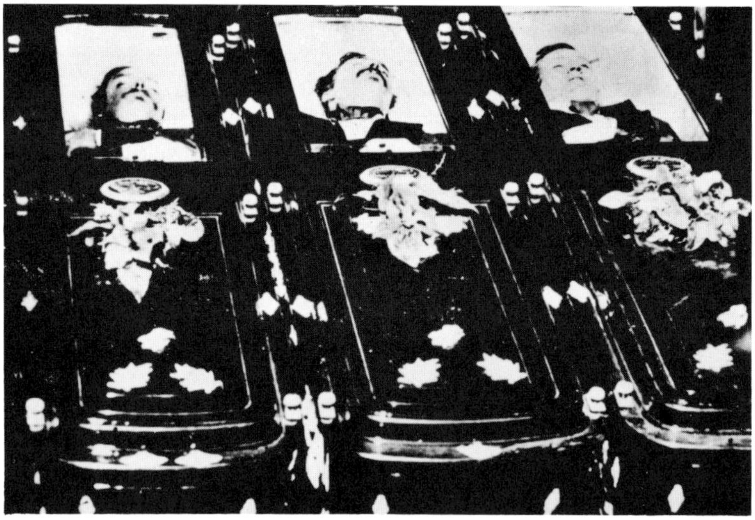

104
The aftermath of the OK Corral. In their ornate, glass-fronted coffins, Tom McClaury, Frank McClaury and Billy Clanton look almost at peace. But anti-Earp Tombstoneites let no one doubt their feelings. Copies of this photograph were sold and captioned 'Murder on the Streets of Tombstone'.

Many years later Wyatt Earp paid an unannounced visit to Tombstone where he took care not to be recognised. No doubt he managed a smile as he stood among the tourists listening to the story of what was even then a legend, the Gunfight at the OK Corral! He died in bed in 1929.

By the early years of this century the day of the gunfighter was gone. No longer was it necessary to hire and fire top-notch pistoleers to maintain law and order. Where once law had prevailed solely because of the presence of the gun, or men strong enough to enforce it, now it was organised on a nation-wide scale. The badmen, too, were no longer able to disappear so easily into mountain wildernesses without trace, for with the aid of the telegraph and the telephone all manner of resources were available to track them down. Civilisation had finally arrived, the Frontier was no more and the Old West but a memory.

But the Old West is far from dead; for to many millions of people all over the world, its multitude of characters are still very much alive.

10 THE WEST IN FILM AND FICTION

When the legend becomes a fact, print the legend!
The Man Who Shot Liberty Valance

The West has been its own best publicist and legend-builder since it was first learned that it was dangerous. The very nature of its composition – arid deserts, vast open spaces, mountains, woods, forests and rivers – beckoned all those prepared to venture into it and eventually conquer it. Early writers played up the dangers to be faced 'out West' and succeeding generations have eagerly feasted upon them. Dime novels added to the legend and became the ideal medium for the 'Western Hero'. Buffalo Bill Cody's 'Wild West' (which he started in 1883 and first brought to England in 1887) captivated audiences eager for the 'cowboys'-and-Indians' West', and by the turn of the century the show had played to audiences in many parts of the world.

Although the dime novel, in modified form, continued to attract a vast readership, it was faced with another and potentially greater rival in the early years of this century – the film. In 1903 in the wilds of New Jersey, Edwin S. Porter produced a ten minute one-reeler which he titled *The Great Train Robbery*. It was the first Western and one of the first true film dramas. From this humble beginning a whole new industry was born, for within ten years motion pictures were big business. The Western film continued to grow in length and stature until by the end of World War I it was an established form of entertainment.

The film also promoted named actors and actresses, some of whom achieved international fame, and Western pictures soon had their own 'stars' (as the fans preferred to call the performers in films), including Broncho Billy Anderson (a bit player in *The Great Train Robbery*); and William S. Hart, an ex-Shakespearean actor who forsook Broadway for Hollywood, and who by 1918 was a household name.

Hart's Westerns are still regarded as the prototype of modern film drama in that they relied strongly on a good plot, pathos, realism, and a sense of romance – the 'good bad man' who, for his sins, became a social outcast only to redeem himself when he put others first or when he died in the defence of others. The sets and costumes, although now dated, were far more authentic than those of later periods, for Hart was a stickler for accuracy. But

105
A still from The Great Train Robbery (*1903*), *the first true film drama made in America and – though purists will cite earlier filmed scenes – the first real Western, for all that it only ran ten minutes. When it was made the West was still by no means tame. Banks were being robbed, cattle rustled and stages, which still ran in remote areas, were being held up. So were trains.*

106
William S. Hart on Fritz in an action shot from one of his early movies. His dress reflects the West of the 1880s and 90s, whereas most of his contemporaries dressed in later styles.

107
Tom Mix and Tony in a typical 1920s Western. He has successfully unhorsed the villain and rescued a lady in distress. He was as flamboyant off screen as on and invented a wildly colourful past for himself, but by any standards he was a major star.

by 1920 many felt that Hart was too dramatic, and the public looked for a more light-hearted approach to the West and its legendary gunfighters and cowboys. It was then that Tom Mix and a new breed of Western star came into their own.

The cowboy figure that emerged at this time, and is to some extent still with us, was a celluloid knight errant who combined the abilities of a cowboy - gunfighter - detective. In place of Hart's stark realism, humour was introduced and fancy clothing appeared giving the whole a theatrical atmosphere. Mix was soon followed by a host of 'cowboy stars' some of whom achieved a 'King' status: Fred Thomson, Hoot Gibson, Tom Tyler, Harry Carey, Ken Maynard, Col Tim McCoy, and perhaps the most beloved of them all, Buck Jones. A further attraction was the star status given to the horses.

Having established a very good formula for what the press jokingly referred to as 'horse operas' or 'oaters', the pattern was changed again in the middle 1930s by the 'singing cowboy', a tradition started ironically as a gimmick by Ken Maynard which was eventually made internationally famous by Gene Autry and Roy Rogers. But by the middle 1950s the singing Westerns were no longer popular and were gradually phased out and are now regarded as freaks by most, but not all, members of the many clubs that specialise in the old 'B' Westerns.

By the fifties, the Western had been established as a major form of cinematic art, some would say *the* major form. The first great modern Western is generally considered to have been *Stagecoach* (1939), and soon leading stars, as opposed to regular cowboy actors, began to appear more or less regularly in Westerns: Gary Cooper (who had been a cowboy in his youth); John Wayne (who had once been a 'B' Western actor and even a singing cowboy with a dubbed voice); Randolph Scott (who eventually specialised in Westerns); Joel McCrea; James Stewart; Henry Fonda; Clark Gable; Gregory Peck and so on.

A minority of Westerns have portrayed the West reasonably accurately, given the demands of entertainment and the eagerness to make the period, and not just the scenery, romantic. The story of the West is epic, not mere romance. Here is a personal selection of ten of the best Westerns, not necessarily claimed to be the greatest, but each of them stressing an aspect of the West better than most of their rivals.

The Covered Wagon (1923).

The first real Western epic. The story first appeared in the *Saturday Evening Post* and was bought by Paramount. Directed by James Cruze, the film was made on location in Snake Valley, Nevada, and many of the extras were local inhabitants. The film was a huge success and for many its depiction of a wagon trek west has never been bettered.

The Iron Horse (1924).

This first classic Western by John Ford depicted the building of the first transcontinental railroad across the United States, culminating in the meeting of the Union Pacific and Central Pacific at Promontory Point, Utah, on 10 May 1869.

108 and 109
The singing cowboy was a phenomenon of the late 1930s and 1940s. The kings were Gene Autry (left) on Champion and Roy Rogers on Trigger.

The Pony Express (1925).
Directed by James Cruze, the film was a worthy tribute to the thrilling, if short-lived, mail service between St Joseph, Missouri, and Sacramento, California, in 1860-1, with its daring young riders who captured the imaginations of millions.

Stagecoach (1939).
Based on a short story by Ernest Haycox, this John Ford classic made a star of John Wayne, and it lives on for its well-drawn characters, magnificent photography, epic duel at breakneck speed between stagecoach and Apaches, and the final sequence and shoot-out in 'town'. That the Apaches would have shot the horses and got the stage has been pointed out by William S. Hart and others, and admitted by John Ford. The legitimate excuse must be dramatic licence.

Red River (1948).
Howard Hawks directed this best of all actual cowboy films. The drive up to Kansas from Texas has never been surpassed in Westerns, and John Wayne gave one of his most memorable performances.

She Wore a Yellow Ribbon (1949).
John Ford's finest cavalry Western, with a jewel of a performance from John Wayne as an about-to-be retired officer and another from that splendidly over-ripe actor, Victor McLaglen. A masterpiece.

Broken Arrow (1950).
Though some silent films had treated the Indian with respect and as a person, this famous

110
The 'King of the Cowboys' in the late 1920s, and until his tragic death in a fire in 1942, was Buck Jones. Here he is having a quiet chat with Silver. Buck first appeared in films in 1919, having been a cowboy, cavalryman, racing driver, boxer and trick rider.

James Stewart film, directed by Delmer Daves, was the first modern film to do so and was therefore a milestone in the history of the Western. Based on an excellent book by Elliott Arnold, *Blood Brother*, it accurately portrayed the extraordinary relationship between Thomas Jeffords and Chief Cochise (the role that made Jeff Chandler a star). It softened the essential savagery of the Apaches (who were hated by most other tribes in the south-west), but it was an admirable and moving film.

The Gunfighter (1950).
Directed by Henry King, and starring Gregory Peck, this film is memorable for its atmosphere and attention to detail, and for Peck's portrayal of the gunfighter Ringo, whose reputation, as age creeps up on him, hangs like a millstone round his neck. He tries to avoid trouble, only to be shot in the back by a kid whose sole ambition is to be known as the man who shot Ringo. Instead of killing him, Ringo's friends let the kid live so that he can endure the

111
De Mille's The Plainsman *was one of the few major Westerns of the 1930s. Here is Gary Cooper as Wild Bill Hickok 'parleying' with Sioux warriors, using his watch as part of a trade.*

reputation of being a fast man with a gun until he, too, is challenged.

High Noon (1952).
Directed by Fred Zinnemann, this classic starred Gary Cooper, who won an Oscar for his Marshal Will Kane, the retiring marshal of a small town, just married and on his way to a new life, when he is confronted by enemies from the past intent on killing him. As has been mentioned earlier, Kane would never in Western fact been left to confront the killers on his own, but this magnificent movie, in perpetuating the legend of the lone man against evil, has no equal.

Shane (1953).
Based very closely on Jack Schaefer's superb novel, this visually stunning film was directed by George Stevens and starred Alan Ladd, Van Heflin, Jean Arthur and Jack Palance. The place is Wyoming and the story was inspired by the Johnson County war, although on a smaller scale than that major confrontation. The brilliant

touches in the film are too many to list here. The characterisations, photography, fights, gunfights and innumerable small touches make this for many the finest of all Westerns. Purists can cite too much of a romantic glow (though not over Palance's sinister, black-garbed imported gunman), but *Shane* is one of the most truthful of all Westerns and a genuine masterpiece.

* * *

It would be possible to list at least a hundred Western films worth seeing, but only the bold would dare suggest that there are anywhere near that number of Western novels in the same class. Until the publication of Owen Wister's *The Virginian* (1902), the form had failed to produce a major work (unless one goes right back to Fenimore Cooper). By the 1890s, however, there had been a move away from the more lurid dime novels, and books began to appear that those who knew the West – as Wister did – could enjoy without feeling they were slumming. Down the years, however, remarkably few first rate historical novels about the West have appeared, but the following are worth anyone's attention, even those who distrust the genre deeply:

The Virginian by Owen Wister
Riders of the Purple Sage by Zane Grey
Shane (and other stories) by Jack Schaefer
Bugles in the Afternoon by Ernest Haycox
The Ox-Bow Incident by Walter von Tilburg Clark (also a fine film)
The Hanging Tree (and other stories) by Dorothy M. Johnson
The Way West by A. B. Guthrie Jnr
Blood Brother by Elliott Arnold
A Distant Trumpet by Paul Horgan
The Log of a Cowboy by Andy Adams

Today there is a growing awareness of how much the West and its mythology are entwined, and the fact that neither can be completely independent of each other. Perhaps that is as it should be, for one surely complements the other.

112
With John Ford's Stagecoach (*1939*), *Westerns came of age and have – at their best – been regarded as a major art form ever since.*

APPENDIX 1

THE QUICK DRAW

Speed on the draw is very much a part of the Western gunfighter's myth. No hero worth his salt is without it, and no villain is expected to survive it. And since the early 1950s there has been a growing world-wide interest in 'fast draw' as a sport. By means of electric timers designed to operate when a button is released, and to stop when the pistol is fired, the modern gunfighter can tell how fast he is: those who 'clock' speeds of less than half a second are considered to be 'lightning fast'! There are also 'walk 'n draw' contests in which two contestants walk towards each other and, at a given command, draw and fire to gain points and a speed and accuracy rating (sometimes wax bullets are used which leave marks).

Target shooters and law enforcement organisations, however, decry fast draw as an irresponsible approach to a very serious and dangerous business, pointing out that few of those who practise it realise what it would mean for 'real', while the cynics sadistically suggest that such people should be issued with live ammunition!

But the quick draw is not a modern myth, for the Old West itself was guilty of perpetrating it. Henry Plummer was alleged to be the 'quickest hand with his revolver of any man in the mountains', according to Dimsdale, and he 'could draw the pistol and discharge the five loads in three seconds'. Others also attributed some remarkable feats to various 'pistoleers' of the time.

Among the most publicised 'pistoleers' was, of course, Wild Bill Hickok, whose legendary status as a pistol deadshot has long been controversial. But there is ample evidence that his reputation as a pistol shot was justified and there are contemporary accounts which allege that his speed on the draw was 'as quick as thought'. An old-timer who lived in Abilene when Hickok was marshal recalled that he once watched Hickok shoot at targets: 'He shot six times so quick it startled me, for his six-shooter was in his holster when I said "Draw".' A Hays newspaper noted in 1877 that Wild Bill was a 'dead shot, wonderfully quick in drawing and shooting, the latter faculty filling his enemies with a very wholesome respect, when in his presence'. It is hardly surprising that with such contemporary praise, the modern day reputations of Wild Bill and other noted gunfighters is so legendary.

But the fact remains that Hickok and his contemporaries regarded gunfights as a very serious business. A man had to steady himself to take his time and place his shots. 'Speed's fine,' they said, 'but accuracy's final!'

Modern tests have revealed that quite remarkable speeds are possible with the old-time single action pistols. Ed McGivern, perhaps the fastest man with a gun of them all, startled the gun world in the early 1930s by demonstrating just how fast one could get a Peacemaker into action.

McGivern, before reliable witnesses, in January 1934, drew and fired five shots into a man-sized target ten feet away in 1.6 seconds. He then drew and fired one shot into the same target in .25 of a second. As an encore he calmly drew and fired, by fanning the hammer, five shots into a target in 1.2 seconds. These last shots were so close together that they could be covered by the palm of the hand. When asked if he would have liked to have been a real-life gunfighter, McGivern said no and that he believed that had he been called upon to use a gun against another man he doubted very much that he would have been able to use it at anything like the speed and accuracy he employed for fun.

In the accompanying sequences we show how the old-timers drew and fired their pistols for safety, and how the few that practised it, fanned their guns.

Revolvers were worn high on the hip during the period of the Old West. Men carried them that way because it was more practical, especially if they were working cowboys. Most holsters were slung over the top of a belt to give the gun butt as much clearance as possible. The now familiar Buscadero 'rig' (whereby the holster fits into a slit cut into the bottom of the belt) came into fashion at the turn of the century and was designed by Sam Myres of El Paso, Texas, based on a suggestion by Captain R. Hughes of the Texas Rangers.

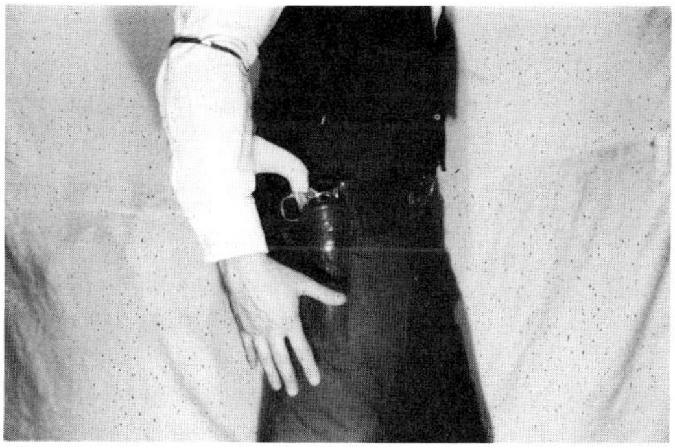

1
The hand is well below the butt, which is worn so that it is halfway between wrist and elbow.

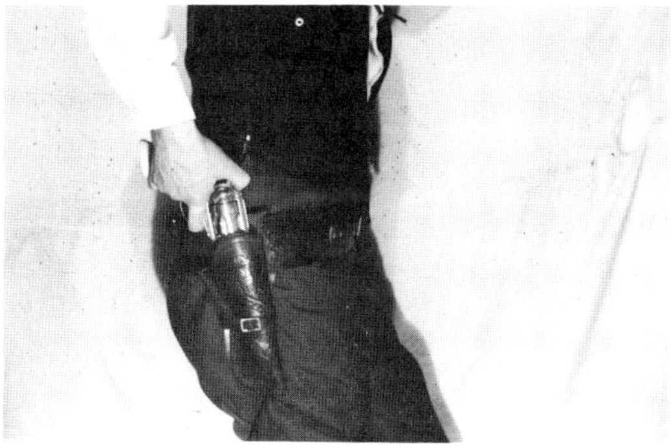

2
The pistol is grasped firmly with the thumb over the hammer and the index finger outside the guard.

3
As the pistol comes forward the index finger slips into the guard and the thumb cocks the hammer.

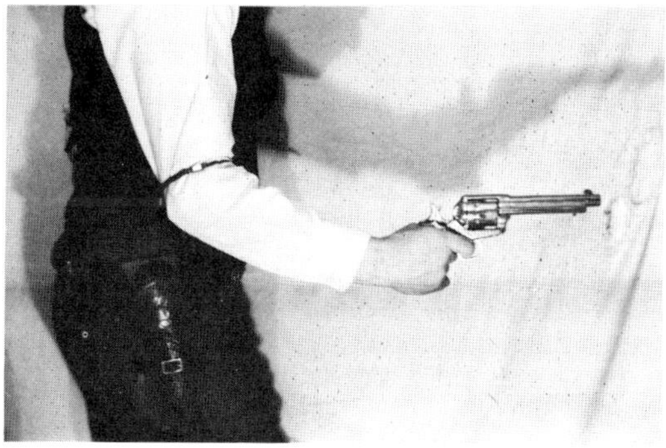

4
The pistol is now at full-cock and discharged as it comes level.

Fanning is the most spectacular of all the gunfighter's methods of getting a pistol into action; but although it is a very fast means of emptying a pistol it is not accurate unless the targets are very close.

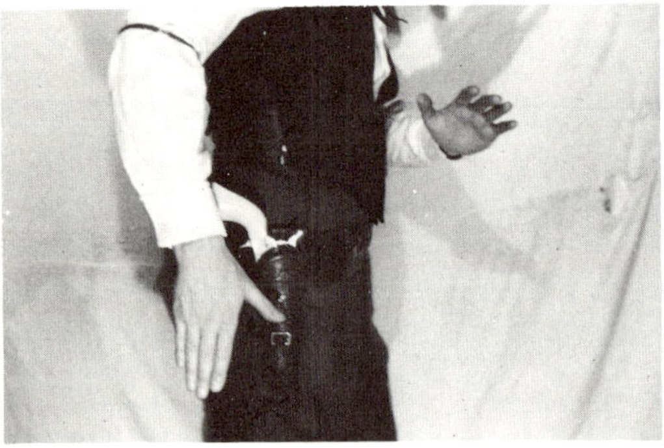

5
The hand is well below the butt as in a conventional draw; but this time the left hand is poised in front of the body.

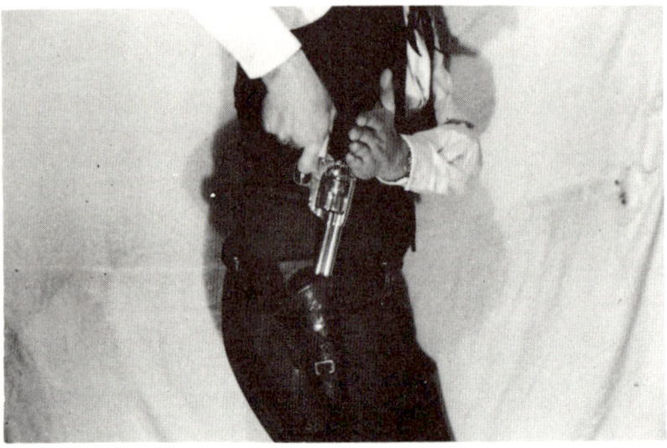

6
The butt is grasped firmly and the index finger inserted into the guard to hold back the trigger, and the palm of the left hand hits the hammer forcing it back.

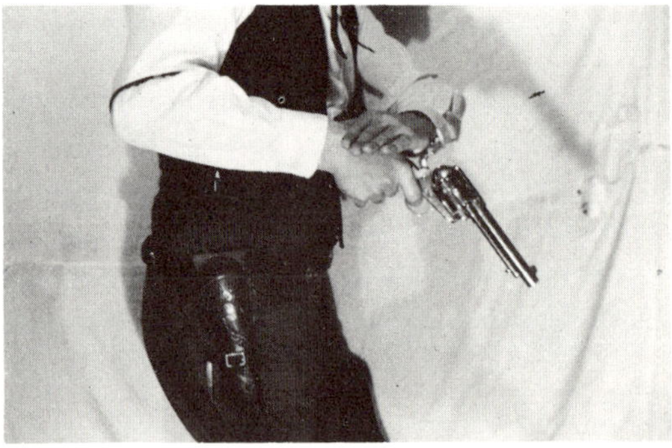

7
As the pistol comes level the hand sweeps back to cock the hammer.

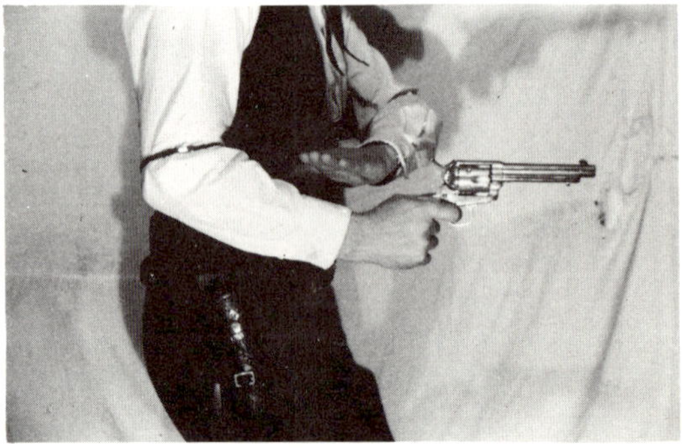

8
As the pistol comes level, it is cocked and fired in one movement, and all the shooter need do now is slap or 'fan' the hammer with the palm of his left hand to fire the remaining shots.

APPENDIX 2

GUNS AND MORE GUNS

The Colt 'Peacemaker' and the Winchester '73 are often claimed as the guns that 'won the West', but, as the following pages show, they had many rivals . . .

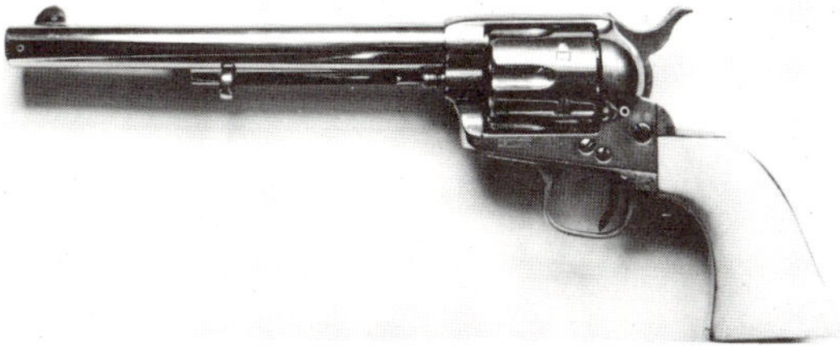

1

1
The most famous revolver of them all, Colt's New Model single-action 'Army' of 1873, better known as the 'Peacemaker'. The version illustrated was manufactured in 1875 and sold through the London Agency, and with its 7½in barrel and .45 calibre is known as the 'Cavalry' model. Weapons in the same calibre, but with 5½in and 4¾in barrels are the 'Artillery' and 'Civilian' models respectively. Natural successor to the 1851 'Navy' as the favourite weapon of cowboys and gunfighters, the 'Peacemaker', when tested by the US Army, was found to be very accurate at 100 yards, and still deadly at 400 yards. The pistol was loaded by means of a gate cut into the side of the recoil shield. The cartridges were inserted one at a time and ejected when spent by a rod contained in a tube alongside the barrel.

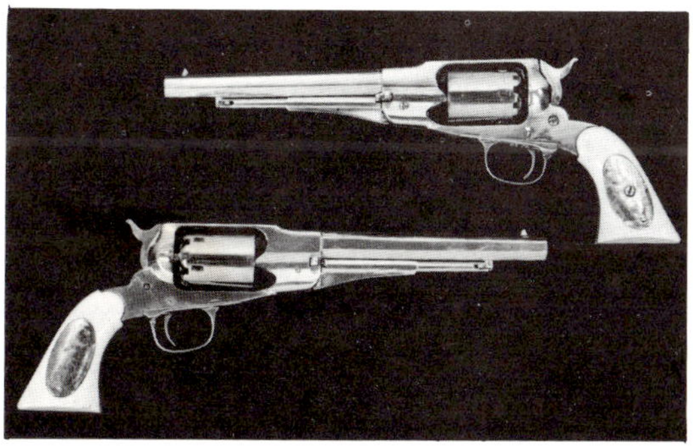

2

2
A fine pair of Remington .44 8in barrelled 1863 New Model 'Army' revolvers, silver-plated and with gold-plated cylinders and ivory stocks marked for presentation, but normal production weapons were blued and fitted with wooden stocks. The 1863 Remington vied with the Colt 'Army' and 'Navy' for favour with cowboys and gunfighters during the hectic years following the Civil War.

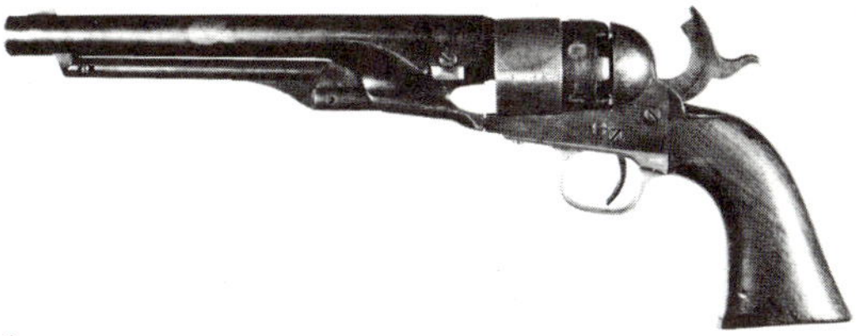

3

3
The Colt New Model 'Army' revolver of 1860. Many thousands of these 8in barrelled pistols were purchased by the US Government for the use of the Union Army during the Civil War. Like its massive predecessor, the 1848 Model 'Dragoon', the 1860 'Army' was in .44 calibre and its heavy lead bullet was also propelled by forty grains of black powder. The 'Dragoon' weighed over 4lbs, but the 1860 only weighed a little over 2lbs unloaded and was a much easier weapon to handle. John Wesley Hardin is alleged to have favoured the 1860 'Army' before switching to a pair of Smith and Wesson metallic cartridge 1869 Model 'American' revolvers.

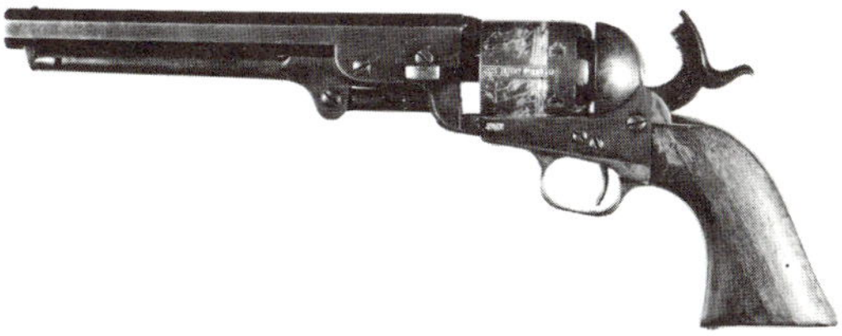

4

4
This fine specimen of the Colt 'Navy' revolver, Model of 1851, was once the property of John Brown. Following the California Gold Rush 1848-51, where these weapons soon established themselves among the miners, the 'Navy' found a new popularity in the Kansas-Missouri Border wars and later featured as the principal weapon of the Civil War guerrillas, some of whom carried as many as six of them in their belts! Although only .36 calibre, these 7½in barrelled six-shot pistols were very accurate and hard-hitting, and were the most popular of all Colt's percussion pistols. It was armed with a pair of 'Navies' that Wild Bill Hickok achieved and retained his reputation as a gunfighter and dead shot.

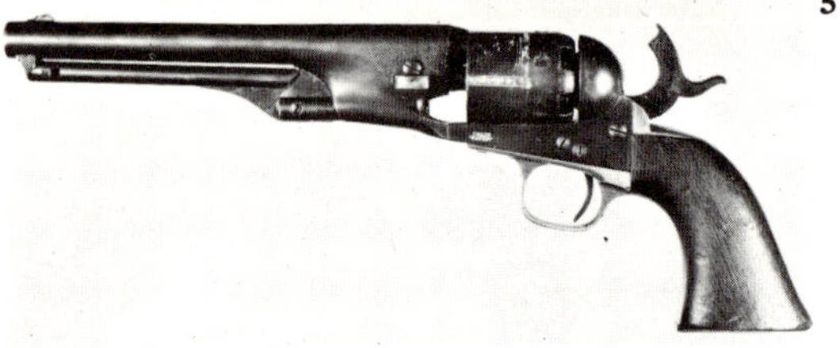

5
In 1861 Sam Colt introduced this streamlined 7½in barrelled version of his 1851 'Navy' revolver, basing it on the new and very successful 'Army' Model of 1860; but somehow it never achieved the popularity of its famous predecessor. None the less, the weapon remained in production until the early 1870s, by which time more than 38,000 had been manufactured.

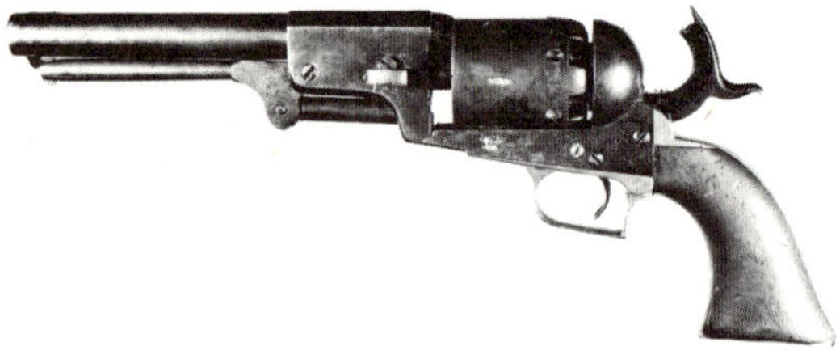

6
An early first Colt 1848 Model 'Dragoon'. Successor to the legendary 1847 Colt-Walker revolver – a massive weapon with a 9in barrel and weighing 4lbs 9oz – the 7½in barrelled 1848 'Dragoon' weighed only 7oz less; but was popular among mounted troops and had a reputation as a 'man-stopper' that few rifles could match! Nevertheless, its weight was its downfall and it rapidly lost favour in the late 1850s. It was replaced by the 1860 'Army'.

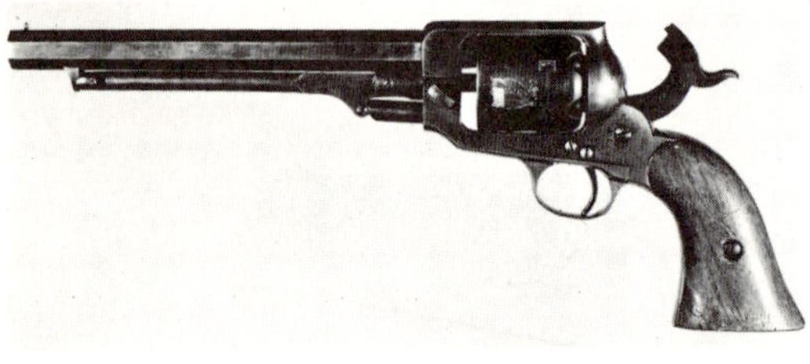

7
This well-balanced, solid-frame revolver is the .36 calibre Whitney 'Navy' revolver which made its appearance during the Civil War where it was purchased in limited numbers. Quite a few of these handy weapons found their way up the Chisholm Trail.

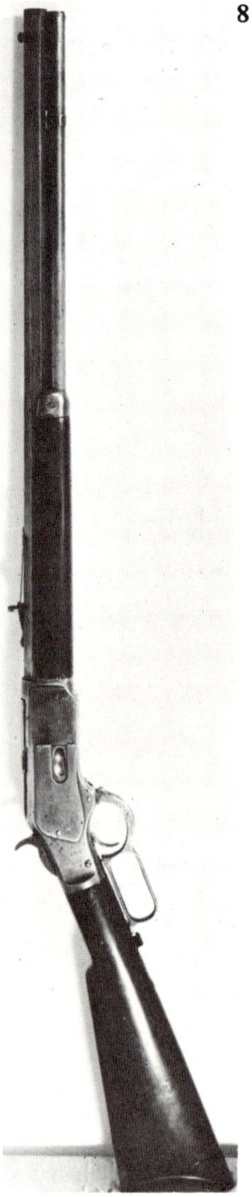

8
The world famous Winchester .44-40 calibre rifle, Model of 1873. These magnificent weapons remained in production until 1924, by which time 720,610 rifles and carbines had been produced. The rifle has a magazine capacity of 15, and the short-barrelled carbine 12. Loading is by means of a slot in the side of the frame, and the bullets are contained in a long tube beneath the barrel. Each time the circular lever is pulled down it extracts a spent cartridge, cocks the hammer, and inserts a fresh round into the breech.

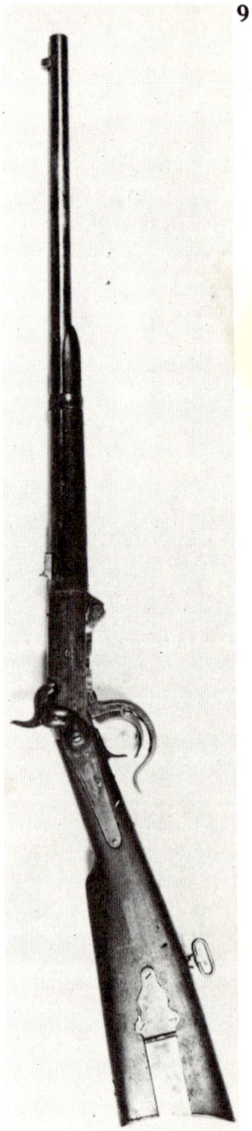

9
The Burnside Carbine, invented by Major General Ambrose Burnside, appeared in several models, including a postwar sporting version.

10

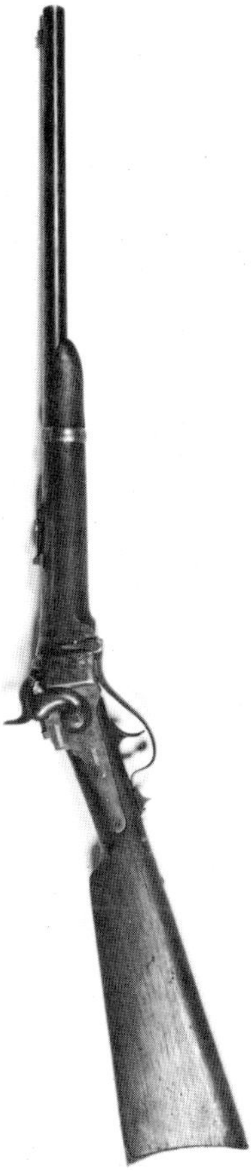

11

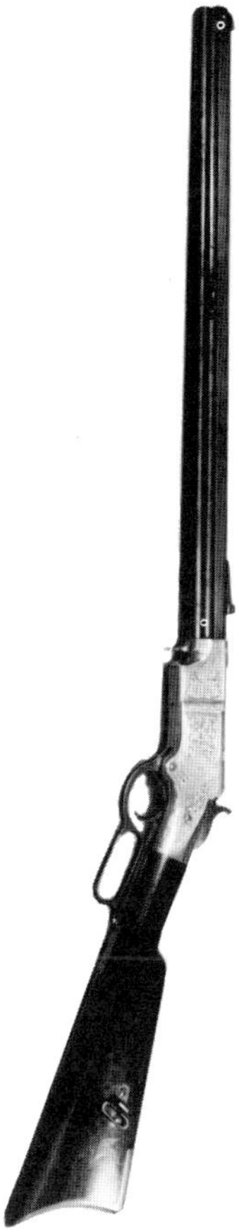

12

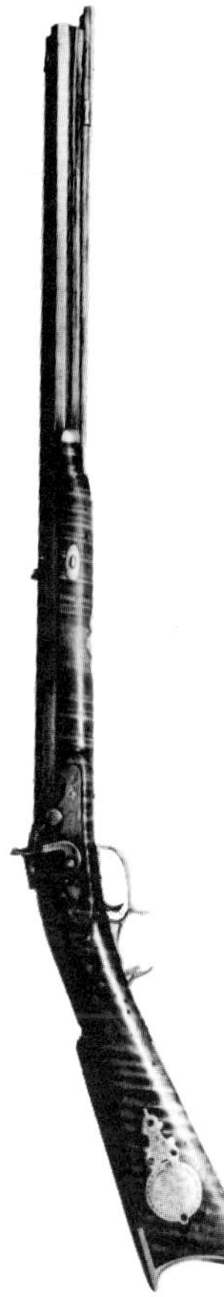

13

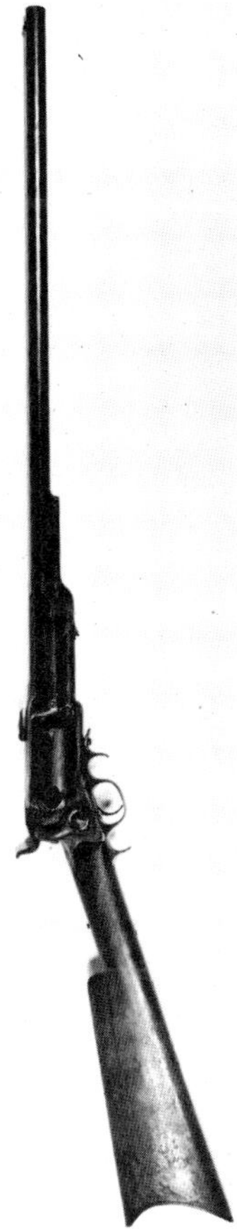

10
The Sharps' Carbine, Model of 1863. These popular weapons underwent several modifications. Some 600 of the 1855 Model were purchased by the British Government; but it was during the American Civil War that it established its reputation as a reliable weapon.

11
This ornately engraved Henry rifle was presented to General James Blunt who had been responsible for the organisation of a number of cavalry regiments in Kansas during the Civil War and also the formation of guerrilla bands to combat the threat of William Clarke Quantrill.

12
This interesting Plains rifle is based upon the earlier Flintlock Kentucky rifles, but is much heavier and compares with the famous Hawken percussion rifles of the 1840s and 1850s. It once belonged to an early Kansas pioneer who used it long after metallic ammunition arms had replaced single-shot percussion weapons.

13
An early Colt side-hammer round-barrelled sporting rifle. Some of these rifles came west before and after the Civil War, but with the introduction of the Henry and Winchester rifles they lost favour.

BIBLIOGRAPHICAL NOTES

GENERAL

Wayne Gard's *Frontier Justice* (Norman, Oklahoma, 1949), though some of it is outdated in the light of later research, is the excellent standard work on the subject of Western violence, while those wishing to relate the gunfighter's West to the Frontier as a whole should read John A. Hawgood's *The American West* (London, 1967). A less ambitious, but fully illustrated work on the same theme is Robin May's and G. A. Embleton's *The American West* (London,

1973). The best-selling *Pictorial History of the Wild West* by James D. Horan and Paul Sann (London, 1961) is a first-rate picture guide to the subject, though the text is very variable.

THE GUNFIGHTER

Though outdated, Eugene Cunningham's racy *Triggernometry: A Gallery of Gunfighters* (Caldwell, Idaho, 1952) is too good not to recommend. *The Gunfighters* (Time-Life Books, 1974) is a visual feast, though the captions often let down Paul Trachtman's informed text. Nyle H. Miller's and Joseph W. Snell's *Great Gunfighters of the Kansas Cowtowns* (Lincoln, Nebraska, 1963) is a masterly book. Other recommended works include Joseph G. Rosa's *The Gunfighter: Man or Myth?* (Norman, Oklahoma, 1969), Frank Richard Prassel's *The Western Peace Officer: A Legacy of Law and Order* (Norman, Oklahoma, 1972), Kent Ladd Steckmesser's *The Western Hero in History and Legend* (Norman, Oklahoma, 1965) and Don Ashbaugh's *Nevada's Turbulent Yesterday* (Los Angeles, California, 1963).

INDIVIDUALS

Though hardly holy writ, pride of place must go to John Wesley Hardin's *The Life of John Wesley Hardin* (Norman, Oklahoma, 1961). Stuart Lake's notorious life of Wyatt Earp, first published in the United States in 1931 as *Frontier Marshal*, and later as *He Carried a Six-Shooter* (London, 1952) has not surprisingly been savaged, but is still full of interest, while Floyd Benjamin Street's *Ben Thompson: Man with a Gun* (New York, 1957) features a less well-known but fascinating figure. Joseph G. Rosa's *They Called Him Wild Bill* (Norman, Oklohoma, 1964 and 1974) is the definitive life of Hickok. Three monographs that typify the best of Western scholarship are all concerned directly or indirectly with Billy the Kid: W. E. Koop's *Billy the Kid: The Trail of a Kansas Legend* (The Trail Guide, Journal of the Kansas City Posse of the Westerners, 1964), Robert N. Mullin's *The Boyhood of Billy the Kid* (University of Texas, 1967) and Colin Rickards' *The Gunfight at Blazer's Mill* (University of Texas, 1974). Thomas Dimsdale's *The Vigilantes of Montana* (Norman, Oklahoma, 1961) is a contemporary account of Plummer and his gang, and a classic.

FEUDS

Earle R. Forrest's *Arizona's Dark and Bloody Ground* (Caldwell, 1936; London, 1953) is the definitive account of the Pleasant Valley war. A. S. Mercer's *The Banditti of the Plains* (Norman, Oklahoma, 1954) is a searing contemporary polemic about the Johnson County war from the settlers' and small ranchers' point of view. There are two major works on the Lincoln County war: Colonel Maurice G. Fulton's *Lincoln County War* (University of Arizona, 1968) and William A. Kelleher's *Violence in Lincoln County* (Albuquerque, New Mexico, 1957).

COWBOYS AND COWTOWNS

Wayne Gard's *The Chisholm Trail* (Norman, Oklahoma, 1954) is the best modern introduction to the subject, while Robert Dykstra's *The Cattle Towns* (New York, 1968) is strongly recommended. Also worth reading are *Cowboy Life: Reconsidering an American Myth* (Norman, Oklahoma, 1975), Editor: William Savage Jr; Stanley Vestal's *Dodge City, Queen of the Cowtowns* (London, 1955); and – on a subject of some interest – Joseph W. Snell's *Painted Ladies of the Cowtown Frontier* (The Trail Guide, Journal of the Kansas City Posse of the Westerners, Vol X, No 4, 1965).

These are just a fraction of books on Western violence and related subjects, and the authors acknowledge the best of them, along with manuscripts and old newspapers unlisted here. Just how vast the literature (which is not always the right word) is can be gauged from Ramon Adams' *Six Guns and Saddle Leather: A Bibliography of Books and Pamphlets on Western Outlaws and Gunmen* (Norman, Oklahoma, 1969). Not all the above are easily obtainable in Britain, though the University of Oklohama books (Norman, Oklahoma) are fairly widely distributed, as is the Time-Life series on the Old West.

INDEX